D1241043

Dante Alighieri

LA VITA NUOVA

THE NEW LIFE

Translated by

Emanuel di Pasquale & Bruno Alemanni

With an Afterword by Bruno Alemanni

XENOS BOOKS

This Xenos Books publication was made possible by a gift
from the Sonia Raiziss-Giop Charitable Foundation.

Cover art: "Dante's Dream" (1852) by Joseph Noel Paton

Cover design: Vorona Weiss

Editor: Karl Kvitko

Library of Congress
Cataloging-in-Publication Data

Dante Alighieri, 1265-1321.
    [Vita nuova. English]
    La vita nuova : the new life / Dante
Alighieri ; translated by Emanuel di Pasquale &
Bruno Alemanni ; with an afterword by Bruno
Alemanni.
        p. cm.
    Includes bibliographical references.
    ISBN 978-1-879378-61-2 (alk. paper)
    I. Di Pasquale, Emanuel, 1943- II. Alemanni,
Bruno, 1938- III. Title. IV. Title: New life.
PQ4315.58.D5 2012
851'.1--dc23
                            2012006659

Published by Xenos Books, Box 16433, Las Cruces, NM 88004.
Printed by TigerBooks, East Longmeadow, MA 01028.

A NOTE ON THE TRANSLATION

The present translation, unlike most previous ones, is in American English and observes American punctuation, not British. It aims at maximum clarity and readability without sacrificing the particularities of Dante's style. References in the work to medieval conceptions of the human body, the calendar and the celestial spheres are explained in footnotes, but the identification of people, places and events that Dante himself chose not to identify are reserved for commentary that follows the translation, so as not to spoil the author's design. Dante's system of literary epithets and personifications is likewise preserved.

A word on the poetry. The work contains thirty-one poems: twenty-five sonnets, five canzoni and one ballad. Dante's sonnet consists of two quatrains followed by two tercets. The lines are eleven syllables each with five beats; the rhyme scheme is abba, abba, cdc, cdc, but may vary. Dante's canzone strings together fourteen-line sonnets, save that each ends with a rhyming couplet. Dante's ballad consists of a quatrain followed by four stanzas of ten lines each; it has a varied number of beats and a varied rhyme scheme. From this short description it should be obvious that any attempt to reproduce these meters and rhyme schemes in an English translation would produce verbal padding, structural reorganization and a distortion of meaning. The translation offered here aims at a literal yet rhythmic version: it maintains an iambic beat, but allows the number of beats to vary. No attempt has been made to rhyme, but rhymes that naturally occur may be accepted. The stanzas are separated for ease of reading. More on these matters may be found in the Afterword.

La Vita Nuova

The New Life

I.

IN THE BOOK of my memory, after a section in which little can be read, there is a heading:

Incipit vita nova.

"A new life begins."

Under this heading follow the words I wish to copy into this small book—if not all of them, then at least their significance.

II.

NINE TIMES since my birth the heavenly light had revolved almost to its starting point[1] when I first saw a glorious lady whom many people called Beatrice, even when not knowing why.[2] She had lived long enough for the procession of the equinoxes to shift one twelfth of a degree to the east, so that she appeared to me almost at the start of her ninth year, whereas I was approaching the end of my ninth.[3] She was dressed in the noblest color—a rich and subdued crimson, tied and adorned in a style appropriate to her tender age. At that moment, I swear, I felt the vital spirit that dwells in

---

[1] The sun, in the Ptolemaic system, revolves around the earth.

[2] Beatrice = "She blesses."

[3] Another reference to the Ptolemaic system of the universe. The significance Dante attaches to the number nine will be explained in Chapter XXX.

the innermost secret chamber of my heart shudder with such force that it ran through my whole body and into the most distant pulsations. With a shudder, it said:

> *Ecce deus fortior me,*
> *qui veniens dominabitur michi.*

> "Behold, a god, greater than I,
> who hath come to rule over me."

Then the animate spirit, which dwells in the high chamber where all perceptions are received from the senses, being amazed, said to the spirits of sight:

> *Apparuit iam beatitudo vestra.*

> "Now hath your bliss appeared."

And last the natural spirit, dwelling in the place of nourishment, wept and said:

> *Heu miser, quia frequenter*
> *impeditus ero deinceps!*

> "O woe, for oft will I
> be troubled from now on!"[4]

---

[4] In the Medieval conception of the body, as described by Albertus Magnus, the vital spirit arises in the heart, the animate spirit—in the brain, and the natural spirit—in the liver. Albertus was an authority for Dante and is mentioned repeatedly in his disquisition *Il convivio* ("The Banquet").

Indeed, from that moment on, Amore ruled my soul, which readily wed him and gave him such authority through my imagination that I obeyed his every wish.[5] Often he ordered me to go looking for this youngest of angels, and I, a mere boy, went looking. When I saw her, I found her to have such dignity and poise that I can justly cite the poet Homer: "She seemed born not of a mortal, but of a god."

And although her image, always in my mind, was used by Amore to rule me, yet it was so perfect and so noble that it prompted reason to give loyal and timely counsel when Amore sought to overrule me.

But since it might seem fanciful to dwell at length on the passions and actions of such early years, I will drop them and, passing over many things that might be taken from the same source, turn to matters that are written large in the book of my memory.

III.

MANY DAYS passed, so many that they added up to exactly nine years since this gentlest of creatures first appeared before me, and on the very last of these days this same wondrous lady appeared

---

[5] *Amore* (masculine gender) is the Italian word for Love. Here it is personified and given the pronoun *he*, which is further explained in Chapter XXV.

again, this time in the purest white dress, walking between two gentle ladies older than herself. As they passed down the street, she glanced to where I was standing awestruck and with her ineffable courtesy, which now is rewarded in the eternal realm, greeted me so graciously that I felt blessed to the very last degree. It was the ninth hour of the day that she gave me this sweetest greeting, and because it was the first time that I heard her voice I was overwhelmed by sweetness, so much so that like a drunken man I fled from the people and returned to the solitude of my room, where, continuing to think of this most courteous lady, I fell into a pleasant slumber and experienced a marvelous vision.

I thought I saw a fire-red mist in my room, inside of which I could make out a gentleman whose aspect would be terrible to others, yet to me was amazingly full of joy. Of the many things he said, I understood only a few—one in particular:

Ego dominus tuus
"I am thy lord."

In his arms I thought I could see a person sleeping, naked but lightly draped with a crimson cloth. Peering intently, I realized that it was the young lady of the greeting, the lady who had deigned to give me her hello. Holding something burning in one hand, the man suggested to me:

[4]

Vide cor tuum.
"Behold thy heart."

Then, standing a while, he evidently awakened the sleeping girl and in his way induced her to eat the thing that burned in his hand, which she did uncertainly. After this, he paused, and then all his joy turned to bitter weeping, and, while weeping, he gathered the lady up in his arms and, as it seemed to me, ascended with her toward heaven. I was so full of anguish that my troubled sleep could not bear it, and I awoke.

Immediately I began thinking about this vision and determined that it had appeared to me in the fourth hour of the night, which is the first of the last nine hours.[6] Reflecting further, I decided to recount the vision to the famous poets of the day. Since I had already learned a bit about the art of writing in verse, I worked up a sonnet in which I greeted all those faithful to Amore, asked them to interpret my vision and described what I had seen in my sleep.[7] And so the sonnet began with the words: *To every gentle heart...*

To every gentle heart and captive soul
who may lay eyes upon the present speech

---

[6] In the complicated system of Dante's time, this is the hour between 9 and 10 p.m.

[7] Dante's sonnet consists of two quatrains posing a proposition or problem followed by two tercets providing an answer or resolution.

and who I hope will give an explanation,
I send you greetings from your lord, Amore.

Of all the hours in the starry night
almost a third part had elapsed,[8]
when suddenly Amor' appeared—
the thought of it fills me with horror.

It seemed to me that he was happy, holding
my heart in open hand, while in his arms
he bore my lady, bundled up and sleeping.

Then he awoke her, and this burning heart
he made her eat in fear and subjugation,
and when he left I saw him weeping.

This sonnet is in two parts. In the first, I send greetings and ask for an answer; in the second, I tell what needs to be answered. The second part begins with the line, *Of all the hours...*

Many responded to the sonnet with various opinions, among them one whom I now call my best friend.[9] He wrote his own sonnet, which begins, *You saw, in my view, all virtue.* It was when he learned who had sent him the poem that our friendship began. The dream's true message was not

---

[8] The night was said to have twelve hours and to begin at 6 p.m., so it is nearly 9 p.m.
[9] Historical identifications of people in Dante's account will be made in the Afterword.

grasped by anyone then, but is now evident to the simplest soul.

IV.

FROM THE DAY of that vision my soul was consumed with thoughts of this most gracious lady, so that my natural spirit was disrupted and impeded in its functions, and soon I became frail and weak. My friends became concerned about my appearance, while others, out of envy, wanted to know the very thing that I wanted to keep secret. Aware of the malice in their questions, yet ruled by Amore in accordance with the counsels of reason, I answered that it was Amore who had done it. I spoke openly, because it was impossible to hide the signs that were evident on my face. But when they asked: "On whose account has Amore ravaged you?"—I smiled at them in silence.

V.

ONE DAY this most gracious young lady was sitting where one hears words about the Queen of Glory,[10] while I sat in a spot where my eyes could see my bliss; between us, in a direct line, sat a woman of very pleasing aspect, who often looked back at me, marveling at my gaze, which appeared to be aimed at her. Many noticed her looking, so

---

[10] The Virgin Mary.

that when I was leaving the place, I heard someone say: "Look how that woman is ravishing that man." At the mention, I understood that he meant the woman who was between Beatrice and myself, and was greatly relieved, assured that my gaze had not revealed my secret.

Immediately it occurred to me to use this gentle lady as a screen for the truth. Soon I was so good at pretending that most of those who were gossiping about me thought they had found out my secret. I hid behind this woman for some months and years, and to make things even more convincing fashioned some little things for her in verse. I shall not include them here unless they relate to the most gracious Beatrice. In fact, I will omit all of them, save for one that can be seen to praise her, Beatrice.

VI.

I MUST add that at the time this woman served as a screen for such a great love—such a great love, that is, on my part—I got the desire to record the name of the most gracious one and to accompany it with the names of many other women, especially that of this gentle lady. Therefore I chose sixty names from among the most beautiful women in the city where the Lord on high had placed my beloved, and composed an epistle in the form of a *serventese*, which I will not include here.[11] I would not even mention the matter but for the fact that as I wrote the *serventese* a marvelous thing happened: my Beatrice's name would not fit anywhere else but ninth in the order of the sixty names.

VII.

NOW the woman who had been shielding my true feelings for so long happened to leave the city and travel to a distant land. Losing such an excellent cover, I was greatly put out, more so than I would have imagined. And, thinking that if I did not say something sorrowful about her departure people would quickly discover my ruse, I decided to fashion a sonnet lamenting the event.[12] I will give it here because certain words actually refer to my feelings for my lady, which will be apparent to those in the know. Thus I wrote the sonnet which begins *O you who pass along...*

O you who pass along love's way
remain a while and try to see
if any bears a pain as deep as mine.
I beg you only suffer what I say

---

[11] A *serventese*—a poetic form developed by Provençal troubadours in which the poet writes as a servant of his lord or lady. Dante's *serventese* is lost.

[12] Here the sonnet form is expanded by the addition of inserted lines and repeated rhymes, making two stanzas of six lines and two of four.

and then decide if I am not
a hostel and a keep to every torment.

Amore, not because I am so good,
but out of his nobility,
put me in such a calm and pleasant state
that often I would hear it said behind me,
"My God, what merit does that man possess
so as to earn a heart so light?"

Gone now is my bold confidence,
which poured out from Amore's bounty,
and I've become so destitute
that I can barely speak.

And so in the desire to be like those
who cover up their lack for shame,
I feign a show of happiness,
while in my heart I moan and wane.

This sonnet has two main parts. In the first, I
endeavor to call on those faithful to Amore through
the words of the prophet Jeremiah:

O vos omnes qui transitis per viam,
attendite et videte si est dolor sicut dolor meus.

All ye who pass by, behold, and see
if there be any sorrow like unto my sorrow.[13]

And I beg them to hear me. In the second, I tell where Amore has placed me, with a meaning that the last parts of the sonnet do not reveal, and tell what I have lost. The second part begins with the line: *Amore, not because I am so good...*

VIII.

AFTER this good woman had left, the Lord of Angels, in his perfect grace, called to his glory a young lady of very gentle aspect who had graced the city of which I have spoken. I saw her body void of its soul lying in the midst of many women who were grieving most piteously. Then, remembering that I had seen her with the most gracious one, I could not keep from crying and decided while weeping to say a few words over her death, as testament that I had seen her with my lady. This I touch on near the end of the following, which is obvious to those in the know. This time I wrote two sonnets. The first begins: *Weep, lovers...* The second: *You villain Morte...*

---

[13] *The Lamentations of Jeremiah* 1:12. Dante quotes from the Latin Vulgate version. This passage became a responsory in the Catholic Church services and was set to music in the seventeenth century by Carlo Gesualdo and others. The English version cited here is from the King James version of 1611.

Weep, lovers, since Amore weeps,
and hear the reason why he cries.
Amore hears the women beg for Pity,
revealing bitter sorrow in their eyes.

Because the villain Morte did her work
upon a gentle heart, corrupting all
that won the praises of the world,
except the honor of the gentle lady.

Now hear what homage he has paid to her:
I saw Amore grieving in true form[14]
above the figure of her body

and often gazing up to heaven,
whither had flown the gentle soul
of this fair lady of such happy semblance.

This sonnet has three parts. In the first, I call
on those faithful to Amore to weep, tell them that
their lord is weeping and say, "*and hear the reason
why he cries.*" This is so they will listen and hear
me. In the second, I tell the reason. In the third, I
tell how Amore has honored the departed woman.
The second part begins with the line: *Amore hears
the women beg for Pity;* the third: *Now hear what
homage he has paid to her.*

---

[14] The words are *in forma vera*—a mysterious phrase that could mean
in human form, or in the spiritual form of those who were grieving.

[12]

You villain Morte, enemy of mercy,
decrepit mother of distress,
of judgement stern, implacable,
since you have given my heart pain,
which I must sadly bear,
my tongue will curse you while it can.

And if by grace I am to bring you low,
I now must undertake to show
that you commit the wrong of wrongs,
not that the people do not know it,
but so that those who place love first
will hate you all the more.

You have deprived the world of grace,
the virtue that wins praise in women,
and from the joy of youth effaced
the playfulness of love.

I will not tell you who this lady is,
save that her qualities should make her known.
All those who merit not salvation
can never hope to share her company.

This sonnet is divided into four parts. In the
first, I call Morte by her proper names.[15] In the
second, addressing her, I explain why I curse her;
in the third, I insult her; in the fourth, I speak of an

---

[15]*Morte* (feminine gender) is the Italian word for Death. Its personi-
fication sets it in opposition to *Amore*.

indefinite person, though one quite definite in my mind. The second begins: *since you have given my heart pain*; the third: *And if by grace I am to bring you low*; the fourth: *All those who merit not salvation...*

IX.

SOON AFTER this young lady's death, something came up, and I had to leave the city and go to a region where the woman who had been my cover was staying, though not quite so far. There were many others to keep me company, at least outwardly, but I found the journey so tiresome that I could not keep from sighing, though hardly enough to relieve my heart's distress, for as I rode I moved farther away from my bliss.

And here the sweet lord Amore, who reigned over me by virtue of my most gracious lady, appeared in my imagination as a pilgrim, clothed in a light and simple outfit. He seemed downcast, looking at the ground, except when his eyes turned to a lovely stream of the clearest water flowing alongside the road I was taking. And it seemed that he called out to me and spoke these words: "I come from the woman who has long protected you; she won't be returning for some time, so I have with me the heart that I ordered you to leave with her, and I'm taking it to another lady who will be your new cover." And he cited her name, so that I knew it well. "But still, if you ever repeat any of the things I have said, make sure that you do not reveal the love you feigned for one that you now must shift to another."[16]

When he said these words, everything suddenly vanished from my imagination, yet Amore, for the most part, seemed to merge into me, so that I rode that day with a changed appearance, thoughtful and full of sighs. The next day I wrote this sonnet, which begins: *When riding...*

When riding on a path the other day,
reflecting on the dreary trip,
I met Amore on the way,
dressed lightly like a pilgrim.

In wretched shape he seemed to me,
as if he'd lost his lordship;
he came up, pensive, heaving sighs,
avoiding others, head held low.

Espying me, he called to me by name,
and said: "I come from far away,
where by my will your heart was placed;

and now I bring it back for a new pleasure."
So much of him passed into me
that when he disappeared, I saw it not.

---

[16] Here Amore speaks in Italian.

This sonnet has three parts. In the first, I tell how I met Amore and how he looked. In the second, I relate what he told me, though not everything for fear of revealing my secret. In the third, I tell how he disappeared from me. The second begins: *Espying me*; the third: *So much of him...*

X.

UPON my return, I looked for the woman my lord had named on the road of sighs. To be brief, I will say only that in a short while I completely made her my defense, so that many people gossiped about it, and not too politely, and I got worried. Because of this vicious gossiping, which sought to defame me, that most gracious being, she who is the destroyer of all vices and queen of all virtues, when passing by a certain place, refused to give me her sweet greeting in which I found all my bliss.

Here I must digress a moment and explain how her greeting worked its virtue in me.

XI.

I DECLARE that whenever she might appear somewhere, I hoped for her marvelous greeting, counted no man my enemy and burned with a flame of good will. At such a time I would have forgiven anyone who had offended me, and had anyone asked me anything, I would have replied only "Amore," with a face clothed in humility. And just

[16]

as she was about to greet me, one of the spirits of Amore, obliterating all the other spirits of the senses, drove out the weak spirits of sight, saying, "Go honor your lady," and took their place. Anyone wanting to know Amore could have seen him in the agitation of my eyes. And when the most gracious one did give me the benefit of her greeting, Amore was no medium to hold back the unbearable bliss, but was as if overwhelmed with sweetness himself, so that my body, completely under his rule, would often slump like a heavy and inanimate thing. Clearly, then, my happiness lay only in her greeting, and often surpassed and overflowed all bounds.

XII.

NOW, to return to my subject, I must say that I was so stricken with pain that I left the others and found a lonely place where I could drench the ground with my tears. After a while, somewhat relieved, I went to my room, where I could continue to weep without being heard, pleading for mercy from the Lady of Grace,[17] and saying, "Amore, help your faithful one." Then I fell asleep, tearful as a child after a beating.

Somewhere in the midst of my sleep, I thought I saw a young man clothed in the whitest of clothes sitting next to me in the room and apparently deep

---

[17] The Virgin Mary.

in thought. He gazed at me as I lay there and, seeming to sigh, said:

Fili mi, tempus est ut pretermictantur
simulacra nostra.

"My son, it is time to give up our simulations."

At this I thought that I knew him, for he had called me this way many times before in my sleep. As I looked at him, he seemed to be weeping out of compassion and waiting for me to speak, so I gathered up my courage and said: "Lord of nobility, why are you crying?"

And he said these words to me:

Ego tanquam centrum circuli, cui simili
modo se habent circumferentie partes;
tu autem non sic.

"I am like the center of a circle, to which all points in the circumference bear the same relation. You, however, are not so."

As I thought over his words, it seemed to me that he had spoken very obscurely. So I forced myself to speak again, and said: "What is it you are telling me so obscurely?"

[18]

He answered me in the common tongue: "Don't ask for more than you need to know."

So I began to describe how Beatrice had denied me her greeting, and asked what could be the cause, to which he replied: "Our Beatrice has heard from certain people that the woman I named to you on the road of sighs was treated badly by you, and since this most gentle lady is opposed to everything bad, she did not deign to say hello to you, fearing bad treatment herself. Therefore, so that she might know your long-kept secret, at least in part, I want you to put certain words into rhyme, telling her of the power I hold over you through her, and how you became hers, right away, even in childhood. And as your witness call one who knows, and have him speak to her of it. And I, who am that one, will freely tell her. And thus she will know your purpose and be able to judge those who were deceived. Make your words serve as a mediator, so that you do not speak to her directly, which is not proper. Do not send them anywhere where she can hear them without me, but beautify them with sweet harmony in which I will be present when needed."

And saying these words, he vanished, and my sleep was broken. Coming to myself, I discovered that this vision had appeared to me in the ninth hour of the day. Before leaving the room, I resolved to write a ballad in which I would carry out what

my Lord had imposed on me, and later I did. [18] It
begins: *Ballad, I want...*

Ballad, I want for you to find Amore
and go with him to meet my lady,
so that my cause, which you can sing,
my lord can then explain to her.

You go, ballad, so courteously,
that even without company
you might endeavor to go anywhere;
but if you truly want success,
first find Amore,
for it's not wise to go without him,
since she who is to hear these words,
if I am right, is stirred against me,
and should you come to her alone,
you might be easily disgraced.

With a sweet sound, while he is with you,
once you have begged her kind indulgence,
pronounce these words:
"My lady, he who sent me to you
desires that you would let me speak
to prove to you he has excuse.
Here is Amore, who can change him
at his behest and through your beauty.
Know then, his gaze was turned upon another,
while yet his heart stayed true."

---

[18] The ballad usually tells a story and can be set to music. Often there is
a refrain, but not here.

[20]

Tell her: "My lady, know his heart is fixed
with such firm faith he has one only thought:
it is to serve you. From the start,
he was all yours, and did not stray."
If she does not believe your plea,
tell her to ask Amor', who knows the truth,
and after that make her a humble prayer
that if she finds she can't forgive him,
she may send word for me to die,
and as her faithful servant I'll comply.

And say to him who is the key to pity,
before you take your leave,
so he who knows my cause will plead it well:
"Amore, stay a while with her,
and by the grace of my sweet notes,
speak as you wish about your servant;
if she forgives him at your bidding,
let her fair smile announce the peace."
My dear ballad, when it should please you,
go at that point to win your honor.

This ballad is divided into three parts. In the
first, I tell it where to go, encourage it to go more
safely and tell it what company to keep if it wants
to go safely and without danger. In the second, I
tell it what it must impart. In the third, I let it go
whenever it wishes, recommending its departure to
the arms of fortune. The second part starts: *With a
sweet sound, when he is with you*; the third: *My
dear ballad...*

Someone might object that he does not know whom I am addressing here in the second person, as the ballad contains nothing more than my own words, but I will solve this uncertainty and make it clear in another section of this little book, a section even more uncertain. So if anyone has doubts now, let him be patient, and later he will understand.[19]

XIII.

AFTER the vision described above, when I had already spoken the words that Amore imposed on me, many and diverse thoughts began to assail and to tempt me, and against each I was almost defenseless. Among these, four most disturbed my peace of mind. One was this: The lordship of Amore is good because it turns his faithful one away from vile things. A second was this: The lordship of Amore is not good because the more faith his faithful one brings him, the graver and more painful the points he must pass. Yet a third was this: The name of Amore is so sweet to hear that it seems impossible to me that his effects in most things could be anything other than sweet, since names follow from the things named, as it is written:

Nomina sunt consequentia rerum.
"Names are the consequences of things."

---

[19] The section is XXV.

The last was this: The lady by whom Amore so binds you is not like other ladies whose hearts are easily moved.

Each of these thoughts so battered me that I became like a man standing in the road who can't decide which path to take: he wants to go, but doesn't know which way. And if I tried to find a general way in the middle, a place where all roads would meet, it was the way most hateful to me, namely, to call on and throw myself into the arms of Pity. In this state, I got the desire to write more verses, and at once composed the following sonnet, which begins: *All of my thoughts...*

All of my thoughts speaks of Amore,
yet each is different from the rest;
the one persuades me by its power,
the other says that power is mad,

another soothes me with its hope,
and yet another makes me weep;
all are atremble with faint heart,
agreed in one thing only—wanting pity.

I know not which is best to follow,
and want to speak, but know not what to say,
and find myself adrift in love.

[23]

So if I want to bring them all together,
I am obliged to call my nemesis,
My Lady Pity, to defend me.

This sonnet may be divided into four parts. In
the first, I declare that all my thoughts are of
Amore. In the second, I say that they are diverse
and describe their diversity. In the third, I tell in
what all of them seem to agree. In the fourth, I say
that, wishing to speak of Amore, I do not know
which part to choose, and if I wish to choose from
all I must call upon my nemesis, Lady Pity, whom I
call "lady" almost with scorn. The second part
begins here: *yet each is different*; the third: *agreed
in one thing only*; the fourth: *I know not which...*

XIV.

AFTER this battle of diverse thoughts, it happened
that the most gracious one went to an event where
many gentle women were gathered. I was taken
there by a friend who thought to give me great
pleasure by bringing me close to so many women
whose beauty was on display. And, scarcely know-
ing to what I was being taken, and trusting a per-
son who was leading his friend to the very brink of
death, I said: "Why are we visiting these ladies?"
He said: "So that they may have a worthy atten-
dance."

In fact, they were gathered in the company of the new bride and, according to local custom, were staying with her for the first meal in her husband's home. So I, thinking of pleasing my friend, suggested that we stay and do honor to the ladies. As soon as I made my suggestion, I felt an extraordinary tremor begin on the left side of my chest and quickly move over my entire body. I leaned back discreetly against a fresco that ran around the walls of the house, and, fearing that others might see my tremor, raised my eyes and looked at the women. In so doing, I saw among them the most gracious Beatrice.

At that moment my spirits were so shattered by the force that Amore gained from being so close to this most gracious lady that all my senses went dead, save for the spirits of my sight, and even they were ejected from their instruments as Amore took their noble place to look upon the marvelous woman. And though I was altered, I felt badly for these little spirits that were complaining: "If this Amore had not shocked us out of our place like a thunderbolt, we, too, might gaze upon the wonders of this lady like our fellows."

I must report that many of the women, noticing the change come over me, began to wonder and to make fun of me with this most gracious one, whereupon my friend, mistaken in good faith, took me by the hand away from the sight of these women, and asked me what was wrong with me. I rested a bit, feeling my dead spirits recover and those that were ejected return to their rightful place, then said: "I have stepped into that part of life beyond which no man can go and hope to return."

Leaving him, I returned to my room of tears where, weeping and feeling ashamed, I said to myself: "If this lady knew of my state, I do not believe that she would be making fun of me, but rather would feel pity." And in this plaintive state, I decided to say some words in which, speaking to her, I would explain the reason for my change, say that I know very well that people do not know it and appeal to the compassion that they would feel if they did. I resolved to say these things on the chance that they might come to her attention. And so I wrote this sonnet, which begins: *You mocked me...*

You mocked me with the other ladies,
not thinking, Lady, what might move me
to take on such a strange appearance
whenever I behold your beauty.

If you but knew, the look of pity
you would not long withhold from me,
because Amor', when I am near you,
becomes so bold and self-assured

that he attacks my frightened senses,
and some he kills, and others he expels,
till he alone is left to look at you.

[26]

And thus he changes my appearance,
but not so much that then I fail to hear
the cries of those tormented, scattered ones.

I do not divide this sonnet into parts, because a division is made only to bring out the sense of the thing divided; in this thing the meaning is clear in the telling, so there is no need of division. It is true that some words could be clearer, as when I write of Amore killing my spirits and only those of my sight surviving, and they outside of their proper place. This lack of clarity is hard to explain to those who are not to the same degree among Amore's faithful, whereas to those who are, everything is perfectly clear. Thus it would not be well for me to expound upon these obscure matters, as my speech would be superfluous to the one and useless to the other.

XV.

AFTER this new change, a powerful thought came to me, one that rarely left me and repeatedly made its argument: "Since you present such a miserable aspect when near this lady, why do you seek to see her? Suppose she were to ask you, what answer could you give her, assuming that your faculties were free to do so?" To this, a second, humble thought replied: "If I didn't lose my faculties and were free to answer, I would explain that as soon as

[27]

I think of her miraculous beauty a desire to see her overcomes me and destroys anything in my memory that might rise up against it. All past suffering does not hinder my wanting to see her." So, moved by these thoughts, I thought of writing a few words in which, excusing myself from blame, I would also explain what happened to me whenever I was near her. And so I wrote this sonnet, which begins: *All that restrains...*

All that restrains me ceases in my mind
each time I see you, beautiful delight;
when I come near to you I sense Amore
who tells me: "Run away, if you fear death."

The face displays the color of the heart
which, as it faints, looks for support,
and in that great and drunken tremor,
the stones beneath me shout: "Die, die!"

Who sees me then commits a sin
unless he comforts my stunned soul,
if only by displaying sympathy

by means of pity, which your mocking kills,
and which the dead look may arouse
with eyes that have the wish to die.

This sonnet is divided into two parts. In the first, I tell why I do not restrain myself from approaching this lady; in the second, I describe what happens to me whenever I do go near her; this part begins: *when I come near to you...* This second part is itself divided into five parts, according to its five different subjects: In the first, I tell what Amore, counseled by reason, tells me when I am near her; in the second, I state the condition of my heart as shown in my face; in the third, I tell how I lose all confidence; in the fourth, I say that he sins who does not show pity for me, as this would afford me some comfort; in the last, I say why others should have pity for me, because of the pitiful look which comes in my eyes, and yet is destroyed and not evident to others, because of this woman's mockery, which leads those to imitate her behavior who might otherwise see this look. The second part begins: *The face displays*; the third: *and in that great and drunken tremor*; the fourth: *Who sees me then*; the fifth: *by means of pity...*

XVI.

AFTER writing this sonnet, I conceived a desire to say four more things about my state that, as it seemed to me, I had not yet made clear. The first is that many times I suffered when my memory stirred my imagination to consider how Amore had changed me. The second is that many times Amore suddenly assailed me so powerfully that nothing remained alive in me but a thought which spoke of this lady. The third is that when this battle of Amore battered me, I went in search of this lady, pale as I was, believing that seeing her would protect me from the battle, but forgetting what happened whenever I came near to so much kindness. The fourth is how seeing her not only did not protect me, but in the end destroyed what little of my life remained. So I wrote this sonnet, which begins: *There often comes to mind...*

There often comes to mind the thought
of how Amore darkens me,
then pity comes and makes me say:
"Alas! What person suffers so?"

Amore strikes me suddenly
and nearly chases out my life.
One spirit only stays alive,
the one that speaks of you.

Regaining strength, in hope of help,
all pale and drained of courage,
I come to you with faith in healing,

and when I lift my eyes to you
a trembling starts within my heart
and makes my soul go from my pulse.

This sonnet is divided into four parts, according to the four things narrated. Since they are explained above, I will only refer to the openings: the second part starts: *Amore strikes*; the third: *Regaining strength*; the fourth: *and when I lift my eyes...*

XVII.

AFTER writing three sonnets in which I speak directly to this lady and relate almost everything about my state, I believed I should be silent and say no more about it, nor speak to her ever again, as I had sufficiently revealed myself, so that I needed to take up a nobler theme. And since the occasion for it may be enjoyable to hear, I will tell it as briefly as I can.

XVIII.

MANY PEOPLE had guessed the secret of my heart by the change that came over my face, and some women who had gathered one day to enjoy each other's company knew it well, for each of them had been present on an occasion when I was stricken. As I was passing by, as if led by fortune, one of these gentle women called out to me. She had a lovely way of speaking, so that, as I drew near and saw that my most gracious lady was not present, I was reassured enough to greet them, asking what I could do for them. There were many of them, some laughing, others looking at me and waiting to hear what I would say, and still others talking among themselves. One of the latter, turning her eyes to me and calling my name, said: "What is your purpose in loving this lady if you can't stand being in her presence? Tell us, since it must be very strange." After she spoke, not only she but all the others peered at me in expectation of my answer.

I said: "Ladies, my purpose was once to receive the greeting from that lady to whom you may refer, for in that greeting resided my blessedness, the end of all my desires. But since it has pleased her to deny it to me, my lord Amore, in his mercy, has placed all my bliss in that which cannot fail me."

Then they began to talk among themselves, and as we sometimes see the falling rain mixed with beautiful snow, so I seemed to hear their emerging words mixed with sighs. After they had talked a bit, the woman who had spoken to me earlier said yet again: "We beg you to tell us where this bliss of yours is now."

And I said in response: "In words that praise my lady."

Then she replied: "If you have spoken the truth, then those words you wrote to her about your own state must have had another intention."

Pondering her words, I was almost ashamed, and left these ladies, saying to myself: "Since there is so much bliss in words that praise my lady, why did I ever speak of anything else?"

Therefore I decided that I would always take material for my writing that would be in praise of this most gracious being. And thinking it over, I suspected that I had chosen material too lofty for me, and did not dare to begin. So for days I wanted to write, but was afraid to start.

XIX.

THEN, when walking down a long road next to a very clear stream, I was seized by such a strong impulse to speak that I began thinking of the means I should use. I thought that it would not be proper to speak of her if I did not speak to ladies in the second person, and then not to every lady, but only to those who are genteel and not ordinary women. Then, I swear, my tongue moved almost by itself and said: *Ladies who are versed in love.* These words I stored in my mind, thinking to use them for my opening; after which, returning to the city and thinking for a few days, I began a canzone with this opening and organized it as shall be seen in its division below.[20] The canzone begins: *You ladies who are versed in love...*

You ladies who are versed in love,
I wish to tell you of my lady,
not that I mean to cease my praises,
but to relieve my mind by speaking.

---

[20] The canzone is a song or ballad of Provençal origin which in Dante's treatment strings together sonnets with diverse rhyme schemes and ends each one with a rhyming couplet.

I tell you, at the very thought of her,
I start to feel a love so sweet
that if I then did not lose courage,
my words would turn all listeners to lovers.
But I'll not speak of her so grandly
for fear that I'll fall short and fail.
Instead, let me discuss her gentle state
with you young girls and loving ladies
by only touching on it lightly, and this
is something not to be discussed with others.

An angel cries out in the mind divine
proclaiming: "Lord, on earth today is seen
a miracle proceeding from a soul
whose light shines all the way to here."
For heaven has but one defect: it is
the lack of her, and so it asks the Lord
for her, and all the saints concur.
Compassion only takes our part.
Thus God declares, referring to my lady:
"Beloved ones, for now remain in peace,
your hope shall stay, so long it pleases me,
while one is there who dreads the loss of her,
and who will say in hell: "O misbegotten,
I've seen the hope of heaven's chosen ones."

My lady is desired in highest heaven:
now I would have you know about her virtue.
If you would want to be a gentle lady,
go walk with her, for as she goes her way

[34]

Amore casts a chill on wicked hearts
so that their thoughts all freeze and perish,
and he who would remain to watch her
becomes a noble being or expires.
And when she meets someone who does deserve
to look at her, he demonstrates her power,
for he receives it from her salutation
which humbles him and clears his mind
                                        / of wrong.
She has this virtue by the grace of God
that one who speaks with her shall not
                                        / end badly.

Amore says of her: "A mortal thing,
how can it be so lovely and so pure?"
He looks at her and to himself declares
that with her God intended something new.
She has the coloration of a pearl,
but not too much, as it becomes a lady.
She is the best that nature can produce,
the standard by which beauty tests itself.
And from her eyes, when they are moving,
there fly out flashing spirits full of love
that pierce the eyes of one who watches
and find their way directly to the heart.
You'll find Amore painted on her face,
and there no one can hold his gaze.

Canzone, I know that you will go and speak
to many ladies once I send you out.

[35]

Now I advise you, as the one who raised you
to be Amore's daughter, young and simple,
to ask of those you meet most humbly:
"Direct me on the way, for I am sent
to her with praise as my adornment."
And if you would not go in vain,
do not remain where there are villains,
but try as best you can to show yourself
to women only, or to gentlemen,
for they will send you by the quickest route.

Amore you shall find with her.
Commend me to him, do not err.

So that this canzone may be better understood, I
will divide it more precisely than the previous
poems. First I will divide it into three parts. The
first part is a prologue; the second is the subject to
be treated; the third serves as an aide to the pre-
vious two. The second begins: *An angel cries out*;
the third: *Canzone, I know...*
The first part is divided into four. In the first, I
tell to whom I wish to speak of my lady and why; in
the second, I tell what seems to happen to me when
I think of her worthiness and what I would say if I
did not lose courage; in the third, I say how I
believe I should speak of her were I not held back
by timidity; in the fourth, I repeat to whom I intend
to speak and give the reason why. The second part
begins: *I tell you*; the third: *But I'll not speak of her*

so grandly; the fourth: *with you young girls and loving ladies...*

At last when I say, *An angel cries out*, I begin to write of this lady. This part is divided into two. In the first, I speak of how she is known in heaven; in the second, of how she is known on earth, beginning: *My lady is desired...* This second part is itself divided into two. In the first, I speak of her in respect to the nobility of her soul, relating something of the active powers that come from her soul; in the second, I speak of the nobility of her body, relating something of its beauty, beginning: *Amore says of her*. Again, this second part is divided into two. In the first, I speak of those beauties belonging to her entire self; in the second, of those beauties belonging to particular parts of herself, beginning: *And from her eyes...* Again, this second part is divided into two. In the first, I speak of her eyes, which are the beginning of love; in the second, of her mouth, which is the end of love. And so that every base thought may be dispelled, let the reader remember what is written above regarding this lady's salutation, which came from her mouth, and which so long as it was given was the object of my desires.[21]

Then, when I say, *"Canzone, I know that you,"* I add a stanza as a handmaiden to the others, telling what I wish of my canzone; but because this last

---

[21] Her mouth is not described, but implied by her salutation.

part is easy to understand, I make no divisions. Bringing to light further understanding would require even smaller divisions, but if someone does not yet grasp what I intended, I would just as soon he leave my canzone alone, as I have clarified it to too many already by means of my divisions, should many hear them.

XX.

AFTER this canzone had circulated a bit in public, one of my friends heard it and apparently was so taken by it that he thought I was more gifted than I really am, for he asked me to tell him what Love was. Indeed, I thought it would be a good idea to say something about Amore after having written in praise of my lady. And so to please my friend I decided to take up this subject. Therefore I wrote a sonnet beginning: *Amore and the noble heart are one...*

Amore and the noble heart are one,
as a wise man once put it in his ditty,
and neither can exist without the other,
no more than can the soul forfeit its reason.

For they are made by loving nature:
Amore to be king, the heart—his castle,
inside of which he rests and sleeps,
sometimes a lot, sometimes a little.

[38]

Whenever beauty graces a wise woman,
it pleases so the eyes that in the heart
arises a desire for something pleasing;

and sometimes it remains there long enough
to cause the spirit of Amor' to waken.
Likewise a worthy man affects a woman.

This sonnet is divided in two parts. In the first,
I speak of Amore as a potential; in the second, I
speak of him as a potential realized in actuality.
The second begins: *Whenever beauty graces...* The
first part is divided into two: in the first, I tell in
what subject this potential resides; in the second, I
tell how this subject and this potential are com-
bined in being, and how one is to the other as form
is to matter. The second begins: *For they are made
by loving nature...* Then when I say, *Whenever
beauty graces*, I tell how this potential becomes
actuality, first in man, then in woman, thus:
Likewise a worthy man...

XXI.

AFTER writing about Amore in the above verse, I
had the desire once again to praise the most gra-
cious one, showing how Amore is awakened by her
not only where he is sleeping, but also where he is
absent and has no potential. Nevertheless, she,
working miraculously, brings him forth. And so I

wrote the following sonnet, which begins: *My lady has Amore in her eyes...*

My lady has Amore in her eyes
and makes genteel all that she looks upon;
and where she goes, men turn to look at her;
the one she greets feels thumping in his heart,

his face goes pale, his gaze turns down;
he gives a sigh for every flaw he has;
his pride and wrath are fled before her.
Please, women, help me do her honor!

All sweetness, every humble thought
is born inside the heart of those who hear her;
the one who sees her first is blessed.

The sight of her with just a little smile
cannot be put in words or held in mind,
it is so marvelous and fresh and gentle.

This sonnet has three parts. In the first, I tell how this lady brings potential into actuality with her noble eyes; in the third, I tell the same thing as regards her noble mouth; between the two parts there is a short connecting one, which practically begs for aid from preceding and subsequent parts, beginning: *Please, women, help me...* The third part begins: *All sweetness...*

[40]

The first of these three parts is itself divided into three. In the first, I tell how she virtuously makes fair all that she looks upon; which is tantamount to saying that she induces Amore into existence when he was not previously there. In the second, I tell how she brings Amore into the hearts of all those she looks upon. In the third, I tell of the good she stirs in their hearts. The second begins: *and where she goes;* the third: *the one she greets.*

Then when I say, *Please, women, help me,* I make it clear to whom I wish to speak, begging the ladies to help me honor her. When I say, *All sweetness,* I say the same thing as in the first part, this time as regards two actions of her mouth, the first of which is her very sweet way of speaking, the other her marvelous smile. Only I do not say how the latter works in others' hearts, as memory is not able to retain it or its workings.

XXII.

NOT MANY DAYS afterward, he who was the father of such a miracle as this most gracious Beatrice gave up this life. Surely he went to his eternal glory, as it pleased the good Lord, who did not withhold his own death. Such a parting is always painful to those who are left behind and were friends of the departed, and as no friendship is as close as that between a good father and a good child, and this lady being good to the highest degree, and her father also good to a high degree, as most believe, and is true, it is evident that she suffered most bitterly.

In this city, at such moments of sorrow, women gather with women and men with men, so that many women had gathered where Beatrice was weeping piteously. I saw some of them leaving her house and heard how they spoke of her grieving. I heard the words: "She is crying so badly that anyone who sees it must die of pity." Then the women passed by, and I was left in such sorrow that the tears drenched my face and I had to cover my eyes with my hands repeatedly.

I would have hidden once the tears began to overcome me had I not expected to hear more, for I was standing where most of the women passed by when they left her. And so, as I waited there, other women came walking by close to me, talking among themselves and saying: "Who of us can ever be happy again, having heard this lady speak so movingly?" After them, others said: "That man is weeping as much as if he had seen her, the same as we have." Still others said of me: "Look at that man. He does not seem himself, he is so changed." And so, as the women passed, I heard words about her and about me.

Later, upon reflection, I decided to write something, since what I had heard from these women was worthy of verse. Wishing that I could have asked them questions, had it not been impolite, I arranged the poem as if in fact I had questioned them and they had answered. In this way I wrote two sonnets, asking questions in the first such as I would have liked to ask; giving answers in the second, taking them from what I had heard the women say, as if in reply to me. The first sonnet begins: *"You ladies with a subdued look,"* and the other: "Are you the one..."

You ladies with a subdued look,
your eyes turned down, betraying pain,
where do you come from, drained of color,
the very countenance of grief?

Did you behold our gentle lady
and bathe her face with loving tears?
Please tell me, ladies, what my heart reports,
because I see you go as if refined.

And if it is a place of so much sorrow,
I beg you to remain a while with me,
and do not hide from me how she is doing.

Your eyes tell me that you've been crying,
you walk back home in total disarray,
and now these things begin to shake my heart.

This sonnet is divided into two parts. In the first, I hail the ladies and ask them if they come from her, saying that I believe they do, because they return as if ennobled. In the second part, I beg them to tell me about her. The second begins: *And if it is a place...*

Here follows the other sonnet, mentioned above.

Are you the one who often spoke with us
about our lady, as we stood alone?
You seem to be the same one by your voice,
but by your bearing seem another man.

And why do you lament so vocally,
that you make others come to pity you?
Perhaps you saw her weep and were unable
to keep concealed your painful cast of mind?

Leave us to weep and sadly go our way
(to try to comfort us would be a sin),
for in her mourning we have heard her speak.

She has a face that emanates such grief,
that he who had the will to look at it
would fall down crying dead in front of her.

This sonnet has four parts, each part the voice of a lady making a reply. Since they are clearly shown, I will not go into the meaning, but will only indicate where the parts begin. The second: *And why do you lament;* the third: *Leave us to weep;* the fourth: *She has a face that emanates...*

[44]

XXIII.

A FEW DAYS later, I was badly afflicted in a certain part of my body and suffered severe pain for nine days without relief. So weak did I become that I lay in bed as if paralyzed. On the ninth day, feeling nearly intolerable pain, I was visited by the thought of my lady. After thinking about her for a while, I returned to thinking about my debilitated condition and life's brevity, even when in health, so that I began to grieve for so much misery. Then, sighing deeply, I said to myself: "Of necessity, even the most gracious Beatrice must die."

This thought threw me into such dismay that I closed my eyes and suffered the torments of a madman, imagining the faces of wild-haired women telling me: "You'll die too." Then, after these women, other faces, horrible to look at, told me: "You're dead." As my imagination ranged in this way, I came to such a place that I did not know where I was. I thought I saw wild-haired women, remarkably sad, weeping as they went down the street. The sun seemed to darken, and the stars seemed of such a color that I thought they were weeping; flying birds fell dead, and there were tremendous earthquakes. And in this fantasy, amazed and much afraid, I imagined that a friend came to me and said: "Haven't you heard? Your marvelous lady has departed this world."

Here I began to cry most piteously, both in my imagination and with my eyes, watering them with real tears. I imagined that I was gazing up at the sky and thought I saw a host of angels flying up to heaven with a pure white cloud ahead of them. And it seemed to me that they were singing gloriously, and the words I seemed to hear were *Hosanna in excelsis!* This is all I could hear. Then, full of love, my heart said: "It's true, our lady lies dead."

After which it seemed that I went to look upon the body in which this most noble and blessed spirit had dwelt. The errant fantasy was so strong that it showed me the lady lying dead. It seemed that women were covering her head with a white veil, and that her face wore an aspect of such tranquility that it might say: "I am gazing upon the principle of peace."

Seeing her this way in my imagination, I was overcome by such resignation that I called out to Morte, saying: "Sweetest Morte, come to me, and don't be cruel, for you must be gentle, considering where you've been. Come to me now, as I desire you greatly, and you can plainly see it, for I already wear your color."

And when I had seen all the sad rituals that are performed over dead bodies, it seemed to me that I went back to my room and there looked up at the sky; my imagination was so strong that, weeping, I said in my real voice: "O most beautiful soul, how blessed is he who sees you!"

[46]

As I sobbed these words in pain and called to Morte to come, a young and gentle lady at my bedside, believing that my tears and words were caused by my illness, got frightened and began herself to weep. She was a close relative of mine, but, because of her, other women in the room noticed that I was weeping and made her leave. Thinking that I was dreaming, they came to wake me, saying: "That's enough sleep," and "Don't be discouraged."

As they did, my powerful fantasy ended just when I was about to say: "O Beatrice, may you be blessed." I had managed to say "O Beatrice" when, opening my eyes suddenly, I realized I had been misled. Although I had called out this name, my voice was so broken by sobs that the women could not understand me, or so it seemed to me. Nevertheless, I was very ashamed and moved by an admonition of Amore to turn toward them.

Seeing me, they said: "He looks like a dead man. Let's try to comfort him." And they spoke many words of comfort, then asked what had frightened me. More at ease, knowing I had only been imagining, I said: "I'll tell you what happened to me." And I told them everything, from beginning to end, save for the name of this most gracious lady.

Later, when I had recovered from my infirmity, I decided to write what I had experienced, as it seemed it would be a fine love story to hear. And so

[47]

I wrote this canzone, *A sympathetic lady*, the structure of which is clarified below:

A sympathetic lady, of few years,
who had the grace of human tenderness,
was present when I often called to Morte,
and when she saw my poignant eyes,
and heard me utter empty words,
was moved by fear to weep out loud.
And other women, made aware of me
by this one who was weeping with me,
caused her to go away
and gathered to revive me.
One said: "Stop sleeping!"
Another: "What's the matter?"
Then I escaped from my delirium
by calling out my lady's name.

So mournful was my voice
and rent by anguished wailing
that I alone could recognize the name
that was intended in my heart,
and with a look of utter shame,
I turned to them, persuaded by Amore.
They saw the color of my face
and then began to speak of death.
"Come now, we must console him,"
each gently urged the other;
and often they inquired:
"What did you see that made you low in spirit?"

[48]

And when I felt a bit consoled,
I answered: "Ladies, I will tell you."

While I reflected on my fragile life
and saw how lightly it transpires,
Amore wept inside my heart, where he resides,
so that my soul was deeply troubled,
and in my thought I sighed:
"It must be that my lady, too, shall die."
Then I was seized by such obliteration
I closed my eyes, made heavy by that evil,
my spirits scattered, each one on its own,
then straying, losing consciousness,
and roaming far from truth,
I saw in my imaginings
the faces of tormented women,
insisting to me: "You shall die, you'll die!"

Then in my vain imaginings
I saw pass by me many doubtful things.
I seemed to be in a locale unknown
where women walked along disheveled,
some weeping tears and others wailing,
their cries discharging sparks of sorrow.
Then bit by bit, I thought I saw
the sun grow dark and stars appear,
and then the sun and stars lament.
I saw the birds in flight fall from the sky,
and felt the earth begin to shake;
a man appeared, washed-out and hoarse,

who said to me: "Hey, don't you know the news?
Your lady's dead, she was so beautiful."

I raised my eyes, now bathed in tears,
and saw what seemed a rain of manna,
and angels soaring up to heaven
preceded by a little cloud,
behind which they all cried: *Hosanna.*
Had they said more, I'd surely tell you.
Amore said: "I'll hold back nothing from you.
Come see our lady where she lies."
My false imagining then took me
to see my lady lying now in state,
and as I caught first sight of her
the women draped her with a veil.
Her look retained her true humility
and seemed to say: "I am at peace."

I grew so meek in my great sorrow,
as I beheld the shape of her repose,
that I exclaimed: "O Morte, very sweet
                                    / I hold you;
from now on you should be a gentle thing,
for you have made a home within my lady
and should have pity, not disdain.
See how I long to be among your own,
so much that I resemble you, in faith.
"Come now to me, my heart implores you."
And then I left, the final rites completed.
And when I was alone at last I said,
as I looked up toward the highest realm:

[50]

"Whoever sees you, lovely soul, is blessed!"
You called me then, and it was for the best.

This canzone has two parts. In the first, speaking to a person who is not specified, I tell how I was raised from a vain fantasy by certain women, and how I promised to tell them of it. In the second, I tell how I told them. The second begins: *While I reflected...* The first part is itself divided into two. In the first, I say what certain women, and one in particular, said and did because of my fantasy, before I had returned to my real condition. In the second, I say what they told me after I came out of my delirium, beginning: *So mournful was my voice...* Then when I say, *While I reflected*, I tell what I told them was in my imagination. This has two parts. In the first, I relate in sequence what I imagined; in the second, telling at what point they called me, I thank them discreetly. And this part is: *You called me then...*

XXIV.

AFTER this false imagining, it happened one day, as I was sitting somewhere and thinking, that I felt my heart tremble, as if I were in the presence of this lady. And then I tell you that an image of Amore came to me, seemingly from the area where my lady lived, and he seemed to say joyfully in my heart: "Be sure to bless the day I took you, as you

[51]

should." And in fact my heart was so happy that it didn't seem my own heart, but a new one.

Soon after these words, which my heart spoke to me with the tongue of Amore, I saw coming toward me a gentle lady, famous for her beauty, who had long been the beloved of my best friend. Her name was Giovanna, but because of her beauty, or so people believed, she was also given the name Primavera.[22] And, as I watched, I saw the wonderful Beatrice coming behind her. One after the other, they passed near by me, and in my heart Amore seemed to say: "The first is called Primavera solely for her coming today, for I inspired the one who named her to call her Primavera: *she who will come first* on the day Beatrice will show herself after her faithful servant's imagining.[23] And if you consider her first name *Giovanna*, it is equivalent to *prima verrà*, for it comes from that Giovanni who preceded the true light,[24] saying,

Ego vox clamatis in deserto:
parate viam Domini.

"I am a voice crying in the wilderness:
prepare the way of the Lord." [25]

---

[22] Which means *Spring*.
[23] *Prima verrà*—"she will come first."
[24] Giovanni—John the Baptist; the true light—Jesus Christ.
[25] Mark I:3.

And then Amore also seemed to say to me: "Anyone who considers the matter carefully, noting Beatrice's similarity to me, would call her Amore." Upon reflection, I decided to write in verse to my best friend, thinking that his heart still admired the beauty of this gentle Primavera, but holding back certain words that were better left unsaid. And so I wrote this sonnet, which begins: *I felt awaken...*

I felt awaken in my heart
a loving spirit that had been asleep,
and from afar I saw Amore coming,
so happy that I hardly knew him.

"Prepare," said he, "to sing my praises,"
and in each word there was a smile.
And as my lord remained with me a while,
I looked back up the way that he had come,

and saw them walking straight toward me—
the lady Vanna and the lady Bice[26]:
one miracle upon another.

Then, as I frequently recall,
Amore said to me: "The first is Spring,
the next, so like me, has the name of Love."

---

[26] That is, Giovanna and Beatrice.

This sonnet has many parts. The first of which tells how I felt a familiar tremble awaken in my heart, and how it seemed that Amore, coming from far away, happily appeared in my heart. The second tells what Amore seemed to say in my heart and how he looked to me. The third tells how, after he had stayed with me for a while, I saw and heard certain things. The second part begins: *"Prepare;* the third: *And as my lord...* The third part itself divides into two. In the first, I tell what I saw; in the second, I tell what I heard. The second begins: *Amore said to me...*

XXV.

POSSIBLY a person wishing to be free of every doubt would raise this one, that I speak of Amore as if it were a self-sufficient thing and possessed not only an intelligent substance, but also a corporeal one, which, in fact, is not so. This person would say that Amore is not a substance at all, but an accident of substance. That I speak of Amore as if it had a body, and even as if it were a man, appears from three things I say about it. I say that I saw it coming; so, since coming implies locomotion, and according to the Philosopher[27] only a body is capable of locomotion, it seems that I make Amore into a body. I even say that it laughed and spoke, which faculties are proper to man, especially

---

[27] Aristotle.

being able to laugh, and therefore I seem to speak of it as a man.[28]

So that this matter will be clear in the present instance, one must understand that in ancient times there were no poets of love in the vulgar tongue,[29] but only certain poets who spoke of love in the Latin tongue. Among us, I say, as perhaps happened in other countries, and still happens in Greece, not the vulgar but the learned poets wrote about such things. The vulgar poets appeared not too many years ago, and they are indeed poets, because to rhyme in the vulgar tongue is much the same as to write verse in Latin according to a certain meter.

If we look into the language of *oco* and the language of *sì*, we find that nothing was written more than one hundred and fifty years ago.[30] The reason a few crude poets acquired the reputation of knowing how to write is only because they were the first to do so in the language of *sì*. The first who began writing as a vernacular poet was obliged to do so because he wanted to write to his lady and she had trouble understanding Latin. And this

---

[28] *Amore* is a masculine noun and has a masculine pronoun; thus, in the chapters above, where *Amore* is personified, the pronoun is translated "he/him/his."

[29] "The vulgar tongue"—the language spoken by the masses, the vernacular, Italian.

[30] In southern France the Provençal language used *oco*, derived from the Latin *hoc*, to signify *yes*, whereas in Italy the vernacular used *sì*, derived from the Latin *sic*.

origin stands against those who rhyme on matters other than the amorous, since such a means of expression was from the beginning invented to speak of Amore.

So then, seeing that poets are granted greater literary license than prosers, and that these recent rhymers are nothing other than poets in the vulgar tongue, it is proper and fitting that they, too, should be granted greater literary license than other writers in the vulgar tongue. Hence, if any figure of speech or rhetorical flourish is granted to the Latin poets, it should also be granted to the vulgar rhymers as well.

Therefore, if we find that the Latin poets spoke to inanimate things as if they had sense and reason, and had them speak to each other, and not just real things, but unreal things, and they said of these imaginary and non-existent things that they spoke, and that things contingent on substance spoke as if they were themselves substances and men, then it is fitting that writers of rhymes should do the same, not just for any reason, but for one that can be explained afterwards in prose.

That poets have written as I have said, we can see in Virgil, who writes that Juno, a goddess hostile to the Trojans, spoke to Aeolus, the lord of the winds. In the first book of *The Aeneid*, she says: *Eole, nanque tibi.* ("Aeolus, it is to you.") And this lord answers: *Tuus, o regina, quid optes explorare labor; michi iussa capessere fas est.* ("O Queen, it is

[56]

for you to state your wishes; my duty is to obey.")[31]
In the third book of *The Aeneid*, this same poet has
an inanimate thing speak to an animate: *Darda-
nide duri.* ("Tough sons of Dardanus.")[32]

In Lucan, the animate speaks to the inanimate:
Multum, Roma, tamen debes civilibus armis.
("Much, Rome, do you owe to civil arms.") In
Horace, a man speaks to his own mind as if to an-
other person, and not only do the words belong to
Horace, but he says them as if reciting the good
Homer. Thus, in his *Ars Poetica: Dic michi, Musa,
virum.* ("Tell me, Muse, of the man.") In Ovid,
Amore speaks as if it were human. Thus, in the
beginning of his book *De Remediis Amoris: Bella
mihi, video, bella parantur, ait.* ("Wars against me,
I see, wars are being prepared.")

These examples should clarify any problem any-
one may have with my little book.

And so that some crude person not be em-
boldened, let me say that since the poets did not
write the way they did without reason, the rhymers
should not do so either, for it would be a great
disgrace if someone dressed up his rhyme in a
figure of speech or a rhetorical flourish and could
not undress it in order to explain its meaning, if
asked to do so. My best friend and I know well
those who write rhymes so foolishly.

---

[31] *The Aeneid*, Book I, lines 65 and 76-77.
[32] *The Aeneid*, Book III, line 94. A stone shrine speaks to the Trojans.

XXVI.

THIS MOST gracious lady, of whom I have written above, was so admired in public that when she walked down the street, people ran to see her, which gave me great joy. And when she was near someone, she touched his heart so deeply that he did not dare to raise his eyes, or to respond to her greeting, and this was seen by many who could give witness, should anyone doubt it. Crowned and clothed in humility, she went her way, showing no vainglory on account of what she saw and heard. Many, after she had passed, said: "This is no woman, but rather one of the most beautiful angels from heaven." Others said: "She is a marvel; blessed be the Lord who works so miraculously." What I am saying is that she showed herself to be so gentle and full of everything pleasing that those who gazed at her experienced a pure and tender sweetness in themselves that they could not describe. And no one who did gaze at her could hold back a sigh.

These and more wondrous things virtuously emanated from her. Consequently, wishing to resume my manner of praising her, I decided to write verse that would present her wondrous and excellent effects, so that not only those who could see her, but others as well could know of her what words can tell. And so I wrote this sonnet, which begins: *So gentle and so honest...*

So gentle and so honest is my lady
when she bestows her greeting on another
that every tongue must tremble and fall mute
and not an eye makes bold to look at her.

She hears the praises round her as she goes,
benevolently graced with modesty,
and seems a thing come down from heaven
to show the world a miracle.

Such pleasure does she bring to those who
                         / see her,
she sends the heart such sweetness through
                         / the eyes,
it cannot be conceived without experience.

For when she speaks there moves a
                         / soothing spirit
that goes straight from her lips into the soul,
and, full of love, it tells it: "Sigh!"

This sonnet is so clear from what I wrote before
that it needs no division; therefore, as I let it go,
permit me say that my lady came to such a state of
grace that not only was she honored and praised,
but because of her many other women were also
honored and praised.

SEEING THIS, I wanted to make others know about it who were unaware. And so I wrote the next sonnet, which begins, *All goodness he has seen*, and which tells how her virtue worked in others, as will be made clear in the divisions below.

All goodness he has seen in perfect clarity
who sees my lady walk among the others,
and those who go with her all feel disposed
to give their thanks to God for her fair grace.

Her beauty is united with such virtue
that it inspires no envy in the others,
but rather makes them walk along with her
adorned in grace and faith and love.

Her presence makes each thing sublime:
not only does she look so pleasing,
but others gain respect through her.

So gentle is her every action
that no one can call her to mind
without a sigh of sweet affection.

---

[33] Some editions do not make a new chapter here; others do. We have followed the latter, as the division helps to keep the following poem and its brief preface separate. It may, however, conflict with interpretations of the work that set the poems in symmetrical blocks, in which case we do not insist.

This sonnet has three parts. In the first, I tell to which people she seemed the most remarkable. In the second, I say how gracious was her company. In the third, I tell through what things her virtue worked on others. The second part begins: *and those who go with her*; the third: *Her beauty*. This last part is itself divided into three. In the first, I tell how she affected women, that is, to themselves. In the second, I tell how she affected women as seen by others. In the third, I tell of her wondrous workings not only on these women, but on all people, and not only by her presence, but also when she was remembered. The second part begins: *Her presence*. The third: *So gentle is her every action...*

XXVIII.

SOMETIME later, I began to think one day of what I had written about my lady, that is, in the two previous sonnets; and it occurred to me that I had not written about how she affected me at present, and so it seemed to me that my writing was incomplete. Therefore I decided to write verses in which I would tell how I was now moved by her power and how her virtue worked in me. Not believing that I could write about it within the space of a sonnet, I began a canzone, which begins: *So long a time...*

So long a time Amor' has held me
and made me used to his dominion

that where at first he seemed too hard,
he now rests softly in my heart.

But when he takes away my courage
so that my spirits flee from me,
my timid soul experiences sweetness
such that it makes my face turn pale.

And then Amore wields such power in me
it makes my spirits spin and sputter,
and leave my body calling to my lady
to give me even greater blessing.

This happens every time she looks my way,
and I am humbled more than I can say.[34]

XXIX.

Quomodo sedet sola civitas plena populo!
Facta est quasi vidua domina gentium.[35]

How doth the city sit solitary, that was full of
people! how is she become as a widow!
she that was great among the nations.[36]

I WAS STILL working on the canzone, having
finished the stanza above, when the Lord of Justice

---

[34] This canzone is no longer than a sonnet, as it was not completed.
[35] *The Lamentations of Jeremiah* 1:1. Dante cites the Vulgate version.
[36] The English here is from the King James version.

called this most gracious being to glory under the banner of that queen, the holy Virgin Mary, whose name was always spoken with the greatest reverence by the blessed Beatrice. And though it may be appropriate at this point to discuss her parting from us, I do not intend to do so—for three reasons. The first is that it is not part of the original design, if we consider the prologue at the start of this little book. Second, even if it were part of the original design, my tongue is not able to treat the subject as it should be treated. Third, even if we reject both reasons, it is not right for me to treat the subject, as I would have to laud myself, which is most unbecoming in the one who does it. Therefore I leave this subject for another commentator.

However, since the number nine has occurred often in this account, apparently not without reason, and since that number seems to have played a large role in her parting, it is fitting for me to say something about it, especially as it is consistent with my design. So first I will say what place it had in her parting, and then I will give a reason why this number was so closely attached to her.

XXX.

I NOTE that, according to the Arabian system, her noble soul departed in the first hour of the ninth day of the month; and that, according to the Syrian system, it departed in the ninth month of the year, since the first month there is First Tixyrin, which to us is October. According to our system, she departed in a year that we designate as *Anno Domini*, a year in which the perfect number had been completed nine times in the century in which she had been placed in the world, the 13th Christian century.[37]

As to why the number nine was so friendly to her, it could have been to show that the nine heavens were in perfect conjunction at the time of her birth, for Ptolemy and Christian truth hold that nine heavens move, and astrologers traditionally believe that these heavens affect what happens below by their respective positions.[38]

This is one reason, but when I think more about it, according to infallible truth, she and this number are one and the same. I mean by analogy, as I will explain. The number three is the root of nine, since without the help of any other number it can become nine, as we manifestly see when three times three makes nine. So if three in itself is the

---

[37] By Dante's reckoning, Beatrice died on 9 June 1290—the ninth day of the ninth month of the ninth decade. Here June is the ninth month of the Syrian calendar, day begins at sunset in the Arabian system and the perfect number is 10 according to St. Thomas Aquinas. By standard dating, according to the Encyclopedia Britannica, she died on 8 June 1290—the eighth day of the sixth month of the ninth decade.

[38] In the Ptolemaic system the celestial bodies moved around the Earth in nine concentric spheres or heavens: Moon, Mercury, Venus, Sun, Mars, Jupiter, Saturn, fixed stars and Primum Mobile. The immobile outer heaven, the Empyrean, was the realm of God and divine beings.

factor of nine and the factor of miracles in itself is three—that is, the Father, the Son and the Holy Ghost, who are three in one—then this lady was accompanied by the number nine to make it clear that she herself was a nine, a miracle, whose root was solely the miraculous Trinity. Perhaps a subtler person could see a subtler reason, but this is the one I see and like best.

XXXI.

AFTER she departed this world, the above-mentioned city remained as if a widow, stripped of all distinction, and I, still weeping in this desolate city, wrote to the leaders of the land about its condition, quoting the opening of the prophet Jeremiah, which says: *Quomodo sedet sola civitas...* I say this so no one will be surprised that I quoted these words above as if to prepare for what follows. And if someone wants to criticize me for not including the words that followed this quotation, my excuse is that from the first I intended to write this book only in the vernacular. Yet the words that follow the quotation are all in Latin, so to repeat them here would contradict my intention.[39] And I know that my best friend, for whom I write this, would want me to write him only in the vernacular.[40]

---

[39] The implication is that the letter to the leaders or princes was in Latin. The letter has been lost.

[40] The *primo amico* is identified in the Afterword.

XXXII.

AFTER I had wept long and my eyes were so af-
fected that I could no longer pour out my sorrow, I
thought of finding relief in sad words, and I decided
to write a canzone in which, while still grieving, I
would speak of the one for whose sake so much pain
had rent my soul. Thus I began a canzone with the
words: *The eyes that bear the pity of the heart.* And
so that this canzone will seem more like a widow at
its end, I will divide it before I write it out; and I
will use this method from now on.

This plaintive canzone has three parts. The first
is prefatory; in the second I discuss her; in the third
I speak sadly to the canzone itself. The second part
begins: *For Beatrice went;* the third: *My plaintive
song.* The first part is divided into three: in the
first, I tell why I am moved to speak; in the second,
I tell to whom I wish to speak; in the third, of
whom I wish to speak. The second begins here: *And
since I do remember;* the third here: *and when I
speak of her...*

Then when I say, *For Beatrice went,* I speak of
her, and this section as well divides into two parts.
First, I give the reason why she was taken away;
then I tell how others wept at her passing, and this
second part begins: *Her gentle soul.* This second
part itself divides into three. In the first, I say who
does not weep for her; in the second, I say who does
weep for her; in the third, I speak of my state of

mind. The second begins: *But joylessness and the desire;* the third: *My heavy sighs bring me to anguish...*

Then when I say, *My plaintive song*, I speak to my canzone, indicating to which women it should go and stay.

The eyes that bear the pity of the heart
have paid the final penalty of weeping
and now are left devoid of tears,
so that if I intend to vent the pain
that leads me step by step to death,
my words must take the place of tears.
And since I do remember well the time
that I spoke freely with you, gentle women,
of my beloved lady while she lived,
I do not wish to speak to any others,
who lack your gentle woman's heart,
and when I speak of her, it will be weeping,
relating that she went to heaven suddenly
and left Amore to lament with me.

For Beatrice went to the high heaven,
into the realm where angels dwell in peace,
and there she stays, while you she leaves
/ behind.
She was not taken by the cold,
nor by the heat, as others are,
but only by her great benevolence;
because the light of her humility

[67]

shone through the heavens with such force,
it caused eternal God to marvel,
so that a sweet desire
moved him to summon that salute
and from below he had her brought to him,
because he saw that this distressful life
was unbefitting such a gentle thing.

Her gentle soul with grace abounding
departed from her lovely body
and dwells in glory in a worthy place.
Whoever does not weep when speaking of her,
must have a heart of stone, malignant, vile,
closed off to every sympathetic spirit.
No villain's heart, be it so smart,
can ever know a thing about her
and feel a cause for tears.
But joylessness and the desire
to sigh and die from weeping
will strip the soul of any peace
from one who understands at times
just what she was, and how she left us.

My heavy sighs bring me to anguish
when troubled thought calls her to mind,
the one who made my heart to break,
and often when reflecting upon death
a soothing longing overcomes me
so that the color changes in my face.
And when this musing takes a hold of me,

I am beset with pain in every part,
so that I tremble in my misery,
and thus undone,
ashamed, I hide from people.
At last, alone in my lament, I call
to Beatrice, saying: "Are you really dead?"
And speaking to her gives me comfort.

The tears of pain and sighs of anguish
tear at my heart whenever I'm alone,
and would distress another who could hear me.
And what has been the nature of my life
now that my lady went to her new world
there is no tongue with skill enough to tell.
And so, my ladies, even if I wanted,
I could not tell you truly how I am.
My bitter life torments me so,
and it has sunk so low
that every man who sees my livid lips
appears to mutter: "I forsake you."
But what I am is what my lady sees,
and for her blessing I yet hope.

My plaintive song, go now and weep,
and find the women and the girls
to whom your sisters
once used to bring delight;
and you, who are the daughter of my sorrow,
be gone, disconsolate, to be with them.

[69]

XXXIII.

AFTER I wrote this canzone, my next-best friend came to me. He is more closely related to the glorious one than anyone else.[41] When we had talked a while, he asked me to write him something for a lady who had died, and he made it seem as if he were referring to some other woman who was known to have died. But I, realizing that he was speaking only of the blessed one, told him I would do it. Then, thinking it over, I decided to write a sonnet in which I would vent my own sorrow a bit, and then give it to him as if it were his sorrow; so I wrote this sonnet, which begins: *Come now and listen...*

It has two parts. In the first, I call on those faithful to Amore to listen to me; in the second, I relate my miserable condition. The second begins: *the sighs disconsolate...*

Come now and listen to my sighs,
you gentle hearts, for pity craves it,
the sighs disconsolate that go their way,
and did they not, I'd die of pain.

Because my eyes would be in debt to me
for more by far than they would want to pay.
Alas! They'd have to grieve my lady so
that they'd relieve the heart that grieves her.

---

[41] Apparently a brother of Beatrice. See below, Section XXXIV.

[70]

You'll often hear my sighs call out to her:
my gentle lady, who was taken from me
up to a world deserving of her virtue;

and then you'll hear them deprecate this life,
by giving utterance to the pained soul
that was deprived of her hello.

XXXIV.

AFTER writing this sonnet, I thought of the man to whom I planned to give it as if it were made for him, and it struck me as a poor service, an empty favor for one so close to the lady in glory. So before I gave him the sonnet written above, I wrote a canzone consisting of two stanzas, the first of which would really be for him, the second of which would be for me. To a casual reader, the two may both seem written for the same person, but a careful reader will notice the different voices: the first does not call her my lady; the second clearly does. I gave my friend the sonnet and the canzone, telling him I had written both just for him.

This canzone begins: *Whenever I, alas, remember...* It has two parts. In the first stanza, my dear friend and her relative lament; in the second, I lament, beginning: *And then my sighs acquire...* It seems, then, that two persons mourn in this canzone, one as a brother, the other as a servant.

Whenever I, alas, remember
that I will never see again
the lady whom I miss so much,
my saddened mind surrounds my heart
with so much sorrow that I say:
"My soul, why don't you go away?
The torments you will bear on earth,
which you already find abhorrent,
cause me to ponder in great fear."
Wherefore I call to Morte,
as for a calm and sweet repose,
and say, "Come now," with so much love
that I resent the one who dies.

And then my sighs acquire·
the sound of misery
that calls repeatedly for Morte.
To her were all of my desires directed
once that her cruelty seized my lady;
because the pleasure of my lady's beauty,
when it was taken from our sight,
became a spiritual beauty,
so great it spreads throughout the sky
a light of love that greets the angels
and makes their subtle minds to marvel,
so noble is it.

XXXV.

ONE YEAR to the day after this lady had become a citizen of eternal life, I was sitting and reminiscing of her while drawing an angel on some tablets. So engaged, I glanced to the side and saw some men who commanded respect. They were watching what I was doing and, as I was told later, had been standing there for some time. When I noticed them, I arose and addressed them, saying: "Another person was with me just now, so I was lost in thought." They left, I went back to drawing angels and the thought occurred to me of writing verses appropriate for an anniversary, but addressed to these men who had visited me. And so I wrote the sonnet that begins: *There came into my mind...*

The first stanza has an alternate version, so I will divide the sonnet according to the one version and the other. In the first version, the sonnet has three parts. In the first part, I say that this lady was already in my memory; in the second, I say what Amore did to me; in the third, I speak of Amore's effects. The second part begins: *And when Amore sensed her*; the third: *They went out weeping...* This third part is itself divided into two: in the one, I say that all my sighs came out speaking; in the other, I say how some spoke differently from others. The second begins: *But those that went with the most pain.*

In the second version, the sonnet is divided the same way, except that in the first part I tell when this lady entered my memory, which I do not tell in the first version.

First version:

There came into my mind the gentle lady,
the one the Lord on high deemed worthy
to send to heaven in tranquility,
the place where Mary is.

Second version:

There came into my mind the gentle lady,
the one for whom Amore weeps,
just at that moment when her memory
called you to come and see what I was doing.

And when Amore sensed her in my mind,
he woke in my uneasy heart
and told my sighs: "Be gone,"
so that each went its grieving way.

They went out weeping from my chest
with such a voice it still can send
distressing tears to my sad eyes.

But those that went with the most pain,
returned to say: "O, noble intellect,
it was a year ago you leapt to heaven."

XXXVI.

SOMETIME later, finding myself in a place that made me recall the past, I stood there thinking for a long time and had such sad thoughts that they must have given me an appearance of terrible distress. Aware of my travail, I raised my eyes to see if anyone was watching and saw a gentle lady, young and very beautiful, looking down at me from a window so caringly that all pity seemed concentrated in her face. It happens that when people are miserable and see the compassion of others for them, they themselves are moved to weep, as if in self-pity. So I felt my own eyes want to weep and, fearing to display my wretched state, departed from the sight of this gentle one. Afterwards I said to myself: "It cannot be but that this caring lady possesses the noblest love." So I decided to write a sonnet in which I would speak to her and include all that is narrated in this account. And since the account is quite clear, I will not divide the poem. The sonnet begins: *My eyes beheld...*

My eyes beheld the wealth of pity
that was apparent in your face
when you observed the form and manner
that I assume when in distress.

It then occurred to me that you were thinking
about the nature of my hidden life,

so that a fear arose in my poor heart
that I would show my weakness in my eyes.

And so I took myself away from you,
while feeling tears well up within my heart,
which was so moved by your expression.

In my sad soul I afterwards decided:
"No doubt Amor' is with that lady,
the same who makes me go about in tears."

XXXVII.

WHENEVER this woman saw me, her face filled
with pity and turned a pale color, as if from love. In
this respect, she often reminded me of my most
gracious lady, who had shown a similar coloration.
And, indeed, many times, unable to weep or relieve
my sadness, I walked to where I could see this
caring lady, who by her look seemed to draw the
tears from my eyes. And so I felt a desire to write
again, addressing my words to her. Thus I com‑
posed a sonnet that begins: *The flush of love...*
Thanks to the preceding account, the work is clear
and needs no division.

The flush of love and show of pity
were never caught so wondrously
upon a woman's face when witnessing
another's gentle eyes or painful grieving,

the way they are on yours, when you
behold my grievous lips before you;
and so because of you things come to mind
that I much fear could break my heart.

I cannot stop my wasted eyes
from often gazing back at you
because of their desire to weep:

and you encourage this desire,
so that the wish consumes them wholly;
yet in your sight they cannot weep.

XXXVIII.

I WAS so moved by the sight of this lady that my
eyes began to take too much pleasure in seeing her.
It often troubled my heart, and I considered myself
very low. Even more often, I cursed the fickleness
of my eyes and in my thoughts informed them:
"Once you made people cry who saw your sad con-
dition; now, because this woman looks at you, you
seem to want to forget about it; but she looks at you
only inasmuch as she mourns the glorious lady for
whom you used to weep. Damned eyes, do what you
will, but I will remind you of her repeatedly, for
never in life, but only with death should your tears
stop flowing."

After I had spoken to my eyes this way, I was assailed by the greatest and most anguished sighing. And so that this battle within me should not remain known only to the miserable man who experienced it, I decided to write a sonnet in which I would present this terrible situation. Thus I composed a sonnet that begins: *The bitter weeping...*

It has two parts. In the first, I speak to my eyes the way my heart spoke within to me. In the second, I remove a possible doubt by explaining who is speaking this way. This part begins: *So speaks...* The sonnet could be divided further, but that would be pointless, since my explanation makes it clear.

The bitter weeping that you do,
O eyes of mine, so long a season,
makes other people weep from pity,
as you yourselves have often seen.

And now, it seems, you would forget,
were I unfaithful on my side
and did not trouble you with reasons,
reminding you for whom you wept.

Your fickleness makes me reflect
and frightens me, so that I fear
the lady's face that looks at you.

You never should, except by death,
forget your lady who has died.
So speaks my heart, and then it sighs.

[78]

XXXIX.

THE SIGHT of this lady put me in such a new state of mind that at times I thought she pleased me too much, and my thinking of her proceeded in this manner: "This is a gentle lady, lovely, young and wise; perhaps she has appeared by the will of Amore so that my life may find repose." And at other times I thought of her more lovingly, so that my heart consented to the thought, as if to its reasoning. And once I had accepted the thought, I would think again, as if moved by reason, and say to myself: "God, what thought is this that wants to console me in such a lowly way and hardly lets me think of anything else?" Then another thought would take its place and say to me: "Since it causes you so much tribulation, why don't you want to get away from such bitterness? You can see that this thought is inspired by Amore, who brings the desires of love before us, and comes from a place as gentle as do the eyes of the lady who has shown us such great concern."

So then, having fought within myself many times, I wanted again to say a few words, and since the battle of thoughts was won by those that spoke for her, I thought it proper for me to address her. Thus I composed the sonnet that begins: *The gentle thought...* I call the thought *gentle* inasmuch as it concerned a gentle lady, but otherwise it was most base.

[79]

In this sonnet I make two parts of myself in accord with my divided thoughts. I call one the heart, that is, the appetite; and the other—the soul, that is, reason; and say what the one says to the other. That it is proper to call the appetite the heart and reason the soul is quite plain to those to whom I am pleased to reveal this sonnet.[42] In the previous sonnet, it is true, I took the part of the heart against the eyes, and that seems to contradict what I say now; but there, too, I meant the heart to represent the appetite, for my greater desire was to remember my most gracious lady, rather than to see this one. And though I did have some desire for this one, it seemed slight. Therefore there is no contradiction here.

This sonnet has three parts. In the first, I begin to tell this lady how fully my desire turns toward her. In the second, I say how the soul, which is reason, speaks to the heart, which is appetite. In the third, I tell how the heart responds. The second part begins: *The spirit asks*; the third: *The heart responds...*

The gentle thought that speaks of you
comes often to reside with me
and dwells on love with such delight
that my poor heart consents to it.

---

[42] The idea is that the heart is the seat of passion, need, appetite.

The soul then asks the heart a question:
"Who is it comes to ease our mind
and yet contains so great a power
no other thought can stay with us?"

The heart responds: "O pensive spirit,
it is a new and tender shoot of love
that brings before me its desires;

and all its life and all its strength
arise from those responsive eyes
that care about our martyrdom.[43]

XL.

AGAINST this adversary of reason there arose in
me one day, almost at the ninth hour, a powerful
imagining. I seemed to see the glorious Beatrice,
wearing the same crimson dress in which she first
appeared to my eyes, and she seemed as young as
then. At once I began to think of her, recalling her
in the sequence of passing time, and my heart
began to repent ruefully of the desire to which it
had so basely submitted for some days, contrary to
the constancy of reason. Once I had gotten rid of
this malignant desire, all my thoughts returned to
their most gentle Beatrice. From then on, I swear, I
began to think of her with all my heart in shame,
as my sighs often revealed, for nearly all of them,

---

[43] The image of "martyrdom" is explained in the following poem.

[81]

as they came forth, uttered what my heart was speaking, which was the name of that most gentle one and how she had parted from us.

Often some thought was so full of pain that I would forget both it and where I was. My sighing resumed, as did my weeping, which lately had subsided, so that my eyes seemed like two things that wanted only to cry. And often the long and continuous crying produced a purplish color around them, such as may appear in one who has undergone a martyrdom. That, it seems, was the fitting reward for their fickleness, as from then on they could not look at anyone who might by their expression have the power to evoke a similar inclination.

Therefore, wanting this malignant desire and the fickle temptation to appear vanquished, so that the rhymed words I had previously written would give no cause for doubt, I decided to write a sonnet that would contain the essence of this account. Thus I wrote *Alas, by force of many sighs*, writing "alas" because I was ashamed of my eyes, which had gone so far astray. I do not divide this sonnet, as it is quite clear.

Alas, by force of many sighs
that rise from thoughts within my heart,
my eyes are overcome, too weak
to look at others when they look.

They are possessed of two desires:
the one to weep, the other to show pain;
and often they lament so long
Amore rings them with a martyr's crown.[44]

These painful thoughts and many sighs
produce such anguish in my heart
that pained Amore lies near death;

for on themselves these grievous ones
have written the sweet name of my fair lady,
and many words about her death.

XLI.

AFTER this tribulation, during the season when
many people go to see the blessed image that Jesus
Christ left us of his beautiful countenance, which
my lady beholds in glory, some pilgrims were pass-
ing down a street almost in the middle of the city
where this most gentle lady was born, lived and
died.[45] And as they walked along, so it seemed to
me, they were very pensive; so that, reflecting on
them, I said to myself: "These pilgrims seem to

---

[44] That is, circles around the eyes.

[45] Dante refers to the Veil of Veronica, believed to retain the image of
Jesus Christ's face. According to legend, a woman named Veronica
used the cloth to wipe the face of Jesus when he was carrying the cross
on the Via Dolorosa. The relic is retained to this day in St. Peter's Ba-
silica and displayed to worshippers from a high distant balcony on
Passion Sunday.

have come from far away, and I don't think they've ever heard of my lady or know anything about her; rather, they are thinking of other things, perhaps of their distant friends, whom we don't know."

Then I said to myself: "I know that if they were from a nearby town, they would show some sign of distress as they passed through the middle of this unhappy city." Then I said to myself: "If I could hold them a while, I would surely make them weep before they left this city, for I would say words that would make anyone who heard them weep."

Then, after they had passed out of sight, I decided to write a sonnet in which I would clarify what I had said to myself. To make it more effective, I thought of writing as if I had talked to them; and I composed this sonnet, which begins: *Ah, pilgrims walking deep in thought...*

I said "pilgrims" in the broad sense of the word, since *pilgrims* can be understood in a broad or narrow sense. In the broad, anyone is a pilgrim who is away from his native land; in the narrow, no one is considered a pilgrim unless he travels to or from the house of St. James.[46] One should know, however, that properly speaking there are three types of persons who travel in the service of the

---

[46] The shrine of the apostle James, brother of John, who was killed by King Herod (Acts XII:2). The body was said to have been transported to Galicia and buried at Santiago di Campostella in present-day Spain. Other James relics are recorded elsewhere. See Paul Johnson, *A History of Christianity* (NY: Simon & Schuster, 1976), 106, 164.

Lord on High: they are called *palmers* who go over-seas, for often they bring back palm leaves;[47] they are called *pilgrims* who travel to the house in Galicia, for the tomb of Saint James is farther from his country than that of any other apostle; and they are called *romèos* who go to Rome, which is where those I call pilgrims were going.

I do not divide this sonnet, as it is perfectly clear from my account.

> Ah, pilgrims walking deep in thought,
> perhaps recalling things remote,
> are you a people so removed,
> as your appearance indicates,
>
> that you don't cry when you pass through
> the center of a mourning city,
> as if not knowing, unaware
> of its profound bereavement?
>
> If you would pause and hear me out,
> I know, my sighing heart assures me,
> that you would go your way in tears.
>
> This city's lost its blessing, *beatrice*,[48]
> and words that one may say of her
> contain the force to make men weep.

---

[47] That is, they go to the Holy Land.
[48] Dante refers to the meaning of Beatrice's name.

XLII.

LATER two gentle ladies sent word requesting that
I send them some of these verses of mine. Mindful
of their nobility, I decided to do so, and also to write
something new, which I would send along as a way
of truly honoring their request. Thus I wrote a
sonnet explaining my state of mind and sent it
along with the previous one, plus a third that
begins: *Come and hear.*

The new sonnet begins: *Beyond the sphere.* It
has five parts. In the first, I say where my thought
goes, naming it after one of its effects. In the
second, I say why my thought goes up, that is, what
makes it go this way. In the third, I say what it
sees, that is, a lady being honored up above; and
then I call my thought a "pilgrim spirit," since it
rises up spiritually and lingers there, like a pilgrim
outside his country. In the fourth, I say in what
way it sees her, that is, as having such quality that
I cannot understand it, which is to say that my
thought rises up to her quality at such a height
that my intellect cannot comprehend it. For it is a
fact that our intellect is to these blessed souls what
a weak eye is to the sun, as the Philosopher says in
the second book of his *Metaphysics.*[49] In the fifth, I
say that though I cannot understand where my
thought has taken me, that is, up to my lady's
miraculous quality, at least I know this, that it is

---

[49] Aristotle, *Metaphysics* 2.1.

totally devoted to her, as I often hear her name in my thoughts. And at the end of this fifth part, I say "my dear ladies" to make it known that I am speaking to these ladies.

The second part begins: *the new intelligence*; the third: *When it comes near*; the fourth: *it sees her such*; the fifth: *I know it tells me...* I could make finer divisions and produce finer understandings, but these divisions are passable as such, so I will not.

Beyond the sphere that makes the widest turn
ascends the sigh that issues from my heart;
the new intelligence instilled in it
by sorrowing Amore draws it upward.

When it is near the place desired,
it sees a lady being honored;
so radiant is she that by her splendor
the pilgrim spirit can observe her.

It sees her such that when it tells me,
I do not understand, it speaks so subtly
to the sad heart that makes it tell.

I know it tells me of that gentle one,
because it often mentions Beatrice,
and so I know it surely, my dear ladies.

XLIII.

AFTER this sonnet, a marvelous vision came to me in which I saw things that made me consider that I should stop writing about this blessed one until I could do so more worthily. And to achieve this aim I study as much as I can, as she herself truly knows. Therefore, should it please Him through whom all things live that my life will last a few more years, I hope to say of her what has not been said of any woman. And then may it please Him, the Lord of Grace, that my soul should turn to behold the glory of its lady, namely, the blessed Beatrice, who looks in glory upon the face of the One

> *qui est per omnia secula benedictus.*
> who is blessed through all the ages.

Afterword

Bruno Alemanni

THE INSTANT OF PURE LOVE

1.

ONE DAY in the thirteenth century a little boy saw a little girl and liked her. It was hardly an extraordinary event: little boys had liked little girls in the preceding twelve centuries, and even earlier, and were almost certain to go on liking them in the centuries to follow. Yet because the little boy grew up to be famous, and made much of his affection for the little girl, his first biographer thought it appropriate to recover that day. He wrote that it had occurred on May the First, when an eminent man of the city, Folco Portinari, invited neighbors to his house for a party. Naturally the children came with their parents, and when the latter gathered to have supper, the former found themselves together playing games. The biographer continues:

> Now amid the throng of children was a little daughter of the aforesaid Folco, whose name was Bice, though he always called her by her full name, Beatrice. She was, it may be, eight years old, very graceful for her age, full gentle and pleasing in her actions, and much more serious and modest in her words and ways than her few years required. Her features were most delicate and perfectly proportioned, and, in addition to their beauty, full of such pure loveliness that many thought her almost a little angel. She, then, such as I picture her, or it may be

[91]

far more beautiful, appeared at this feast to the eyes of our Dante; not, I suppose, for the first time, but for the first time with power to inspire him with love. And he, though still a child, received the lovely image of her into his heart with so great affection that it never left him from that day forward so long as he lived.[50]

Such as I picture her. With this parenthetical remark, the biographer, Giovanni Boccaccio (1313-1375), reveals that he really did not know how she looked or exactly how the boy and girl met, though he knew the girl's full name and the place and the time. He lived in the first generation after his subject, Dante Alighieri (1265-1321), and had access to people who knew the man personally. These included two friends of Dante's exile in Ravenna, the son of his sister and the second cousin of Beatrice. On one occasion, recorded in the year 1350, he was commissioned to carry ten florins of gold to Dante's daughter, who had taken vows and lived in a convent in Ravenna. No doubt he spoke to other people as well who recalled the great poet. Nevertheless, his account remains very general and largely imagined.

Why does he suppose that Dante and Beatrice had seen each other before the May Day party? Probably because he had learned, as scholars have since established, that the Alighieris and the Portinaris both lived in the San Piero Maggiore district of Florence, and between their houses stood the Santa Margherita, a little church serving both

---

[50] Giovanni Boccaccio, *Vita di Dante*, translated by James Robinson Smith, reprinted in Charles Allen Dinsmore, *Aids to the Study of Dante* (Boston & New York: Houghton, Mifflin & Co., 1903), 77-78.

families. So Dante might have seen her there, praying with her mother and nanny. (See Chapter V.) In any event, according to his own account, he was stricken by the first sight of her, dressed in red, and felt a superior force come over him. Afterward, he would go out looking for her, hoping to get a glimpse of her. Since she would not be free to wander on her own, but would always be kept under adult supervision, he probably walked past her house, a large palazzo at No. 4 Via del Corso, the main thoroughfare. But again, there is nothing extraordinary in all this.

Nine years passed, according to the poet, and he saw her again. Now she was a young lady dressed in white walking down the street in the company of two lady chaperones. She saw him looking at her, turned and gave him a greeting. The ineffable grace and beauty of the moment struck him; his reaction was out of proportion to the incident; his senses were shattered, his mind deranged, his ability to walk and to converse with others was impaired; he had to run away to his room and collapse, to sigh and fantasize about her. Again, nothing special. It happens to every kid.

Yet we might wonder why his reaction was so strong. *Nine years had passed.* He had seen a vision of beauty in childhood and now saw its transformation in youth. The boy and girl, we moderns must think, had passed through puberty. Their hormones were flowing, testosterone and estrogen levels were elevated, the sexual instinct was aroused. Dante, and the Italian Renaissance for that matter, were well aware of animal passions, but did not have the scientific terms we have to explain them. They had to rely on the concepts of their time: spirits of the body, orbits of the celestial spheres, abstract forces like destiny and fortune. Which, making the necessary changes in terminology, are not so different from our scientific props, since we do not really know why hormones and instincts act as they do.

There is another factor that would have been acting on Dante, one that he neglects to mention. It is best revealed within the sequence of these mundane events, which scholars have dutifully dated. Dante was born in Florence in May or June of 1265, and Beatrice was born later in the same year. It is generally accepted that Folco Portinari gave his springtime celebration for his neighbors on 1 May 1274, when Dante and Beatrice were both about nine. Less than three years later, on 9 February 1277, when Dante was eleven, his father betrothed him to Gemma Donati, a little rich girl one year younger. R. W. B. Lewis tells us, in his popular short biography of Dante, that the girl's father, Manetto Donati, owned buildings up and down the Via del Corso, and one of his houses adjoined the one in which Dante was born. Donati and Dante's father, Alighiero di Bellincione d'Alighiero, owned farmlands together and had other family connections. Gemma brought a large dowry to the pact and had a ring put on her finger. Everything was done by the book.[51]

Young Dante, of course, had no say in the matter. Lewis informs us that within the conventions of the time, when families formed armies and waged war on one another, aligning themselves with the parties of the Ghibellines and the Guelphs, the first party siding chiefly with the nobles and German emperors, the second chiefly with the tradesmen and the Roman Pope, these parties on occasion killing each other and pillaging each other's properties and tearing down

---

[51] R. W. B. Lewis, *Dante: A Life* (New York: Penguin, 2009), 26-27.

whole blocks of buildings,—within such conventions, the breaking of a marriage contract would have been a touchy affair. Alighiero was a supporter of the Guelphs; the Donatis were the most powerful family in the body that constituted the Guelphs. Dante, in short, was committed.

Whether he continued to run up the Via del Corso hoping to catch sight of Beatrice we do not know. Whether he had ceremonial meetings with little Gemma we do not know. What he tells us is that nine years to the day after his first sight of Beatrice, which, judging by the foregoing, would be on 1 May 1283, or six years and three months after his commitment to another, he saw her again, gliding down the street in white. Unexpectedly she turned and gave him a greeting, which, given the presence of two chaperones, must have signaled an independence of mind and a personal favor. He felt blessed, and yet, in his unfree state, condemned. The girl that first charmed him and now spoke to him has become the young woman he cannot have. He cannot try to pass messages to her, court her or hope for her hand. He retreats to his room and falls into a delirium in which he sees her unintentionally consuming his heart.

And yet, coming out of it, he finds a remedy for his distress. He decides to write a poem about his experience and to submit it to the judgement of the noted poets of the day. Here was a way to deal with an impossible love—to use it as a basis for poetry. Of course, it would mean stepping into a trap—the tantalizing trap of *fin'amor* ("fine love"), as the troubadours called it. We know it by its later, 19th-century term: "courtly love."

Possibly for the lover who wanted, despite all obstacles, to possess his beloved, it was not conceived as a trap, but rather as a technique that might ultimately persuade the lady to consent to an illicit affair. But for a new breed of poet, courtly love was taken in earnest. The state of unfulfilled desire, prolonged and possibly permanent, became one of intensified feeling, heightened awareness, spiritual exaltation. The adepts of this kind of love became a sort of secret society; they wrote poetry and sang songs in praise of their lady, the peerless one who kept them forever on edge, judged their attempts to win her favor and by her grace and beauty commanded their obedience, compelling them to worship her, to swear oaths of fealty and to serve her as a vassal. In their slavery they experienced a rapture that transported them to the limits of their sensibilities; in their self-denial—to the purest degree of chaste adoration. A. N. Wilson, in his revelatory and often witty biography, *Dante in Love*, compares their state to Tantric sex.[52]

Bound though they were, frustrated though they were, these Platonic lovers obtained a fantastic liberty, for their love would not be confined to social classes or conventions; they might turn their eyes on a married woman or a woman above their class, and yet declare themselves to be worthy, to possess nobility of character, or to aspire to such a worth. Their love, though slavish, was largely their own possession, possibly their own invention. It raised them above the animality of the masses; it ennobled and educated them to attain the highest levels of sensitivity and understanding. It created a society of refined men dedicated to Love, one in which the beloved lady might be complicit, hence a relationship of a

---

[52] A. N. Wilson, *Dante in Love* (New York: Farrar, Straus & Giroux, 2011),chap. 7.

sort could be formed between the lowly knight, merchant, or gardener, and the lady of the castle, manor, or estate. These lovers were obliged to operate in secret, outside the conventions of society in a special realm of pure and superior love.

And while the foregoing description, with castles and manors and ladies, may seem dated, the classical scholar Frederick W. Locke, in a brief but trenchant introduction to a little book on courtly love, points out that precisely this kind of love marked the transition from classical and medieval attitudes to the romantic love of modern times. "For when a passionate lover obediently subjects himself to the beloved lady as to his 'mistress,'" writes Locke, "he grants to this lady a status which women simply did not enjoy either in Antiquity or in the early Middle Ages." The old world of battle, physical competition and sport, in which male companionship was the ideal relationship and women served only to relieve sexual need, produce children and mind the house, had changed. In the new world women became the arbiters of love and offered the lover a transcendent experience.[53]

The new trend began with the Provençal troubadours of 12th-century France, migrated in mid-13th century to Sicily and the court of the Holy Roman Emperor, King Frederick II, and found its mature expression in the late 13th-century poets of Tuscany, who wrote in the *dolce stil nuovo*—the

---

[53] F. W. Locke, "Introduction" to Andreas Capellanus, *The Art of Courtly Love*, edited and abridged (New York: Frederick Ungar, 1957-1978), iii-vii. The term "courtly love" was coined in the 19th century by the French medievalist Gaston Paris. The full version of Capellanus is: *The Art of Courtly Love*, translated by John Jay Parry (New York: Columbia University Press, 1960).

"sweet new style." Dante had two masters before him, masters who would give him a start in a literary career that would take him far beyond them. The first was Guido Guinizelli (c. 1230-1275), the "wise man" mentioned in Section XX of the *Vita*, whose "ditty" practically lays out a program for the new style and new philosophy of love. Here is the beginning in a rhyming translation by Lorna di' Lucchi (1922):

> Within the gentle heart abideth Love,
> As doth a bird within green forest glade,
> Neither before the gentle heart was Love,
> Nor Love ere gentle heart by Nature made.
> Created was the sun,
> And lo, his radiance everywhere held sway,
> Nor was before the sun;
> Love doth unto all gentleness aspire,
> And in the self-same way
> Doth clarity unto clear flame of fire.

Love is made a moving force in nature and manifests itself in the gentle heart—*il cor gentil*—to which Dante refers in the first line he wrote after his delirium. The bearer of love, like a heavenly body transmitting the rays of the sun, is presented in the second stanza of Guinizelli's poem:

> Love's fire is kindled in the gentle heart,
> As virtue is within the precious stone;
> From out the star no glory doth depart
> Until made gentle by the sun alone.
> When the sun hath drawn forth

[98]

By his own strength all that which is not meet,
The star doth prove its worth.
Thus to the heart, by Nature fashioned so
Gentle and pure and sweet,
The love of woman like a star doth go.[54]

The remaining stanzas of the canzone bring in the lady's fine qualities and her relationship to the angels and God. The themes are there for Dante's taking.

Guinizelli has another fine poem, a sonnet, which describes the effects the lady produces on her surroundings. The theme will immediately be recognized by the reader of the *Vita*:

In verity I'd sing my lady's praise,
With rose and lily-flower her face compare:
Like to the morning star her beauty's rays,
Like to a saint in heaven, ah, wond'rous fair!
Green shades are like her and the breeze as well,
All hues, all blossoms, flushed and pale, beside
Silver and gold and rare stones' lustrous spell;
Even Love himself in her is glorified.

She goes her way so gentle and so sweet,
Pride falls in whomsoever she doth meet,
Worthless the heart which scorneth such delight!
Ungentle folk may not endure her sight,

---

[54] *Al cor gentil ripara sempre amore,* from *An Anthology of Italian Poems 13th-19th Century*, selected and translated by Lorna de' Lucchi (New York: Alfred A. Knopf, 1922), 28-32, 348. Available online at: http://www.elfinspell.com/GuidoGuinizelliPoems.html/.

[99]

And a still greater virtue I aver:
No man thinks ill hath he but looked on her.[55]

Thus a connection is made between God, sun, the lady, beauty's rays, the gentle heart and all the people who may see her and be transformed. Dante took Guinizelli's themes, as did other poets of his time, and improved upon them. The reader may compare this poem with the sonnets in chapters XXI, XXVI and XXVII of the *Vita* and see how Dante personalizes his story and gives it realistic touches. In Erich Auerbach's analysis, he develops a logical narrative that is absent from the work of his contemporaries and the earlier troubadours as well, creating a foundation for realism in European literature.[56]

The second poet—another, younger Guido—is one of those to whom Dante sent his first poem: Guido Cavalcanti (c. 1250-1300). He was an established poet, and like Dante involved in Florentine politics. Tragically, he was banished from his native Florence and died of fever on his return home. Dante was unfortunately entangled in the affair. Wilson tells the story. Translations of Cavalcanti's poems can be read online.

Dante cites only the first line of Cavalcanti's response, but it was sufficient for scholars to locate the complete sonnet. Ezra Pound's blank verse translation (1912) reads:

Thou sawest, it seems to me, all things availing,
And every joy that ever good man feeleth.

---

[55] *Voglio del ver la mia donna laudare,* from *An Anthology of Italian Poems 13th-19th Century*, trans. by Lorna de' Lucchi (1922), 28-32, 348.
[56] Erich Auerbach, *Dante: Poet of the Secular World* (1929), translated by Ralph Manheim (New York Review Books, 2007), Chap. II.

Thou wast in proof of that lord valorous
Who through sheer honour lords it o'er the world.
Thou livest in a place where baseness dieth,
And holdest reason in the piteous mind:
So gently move the people in this sleep
That the heart bears it 'thout the feel of grief.

Love bore away thy heart, because in his sight
Was Death grown clamorous for one thou lovest,
Love fed her with thy heart in dread of this,
Then, when it seemed to thee he left in sadness,
A dear dream was it which was there completed,
Seeing it contrary came conquering.[57]

The first line in Italian—*Vedesti al mio parere ogni valore*—is practically impossible to translate, not because it is hard, but because so much meaning is packed into the last two words, which mean "all valour, all value, all virtue, all merit, all worth." The translator can choose only one of these options, but wants to include them all. The last line, however, is obscure. Apparently it refers to a belief that toward dawn dreams portray the opposite of reality. Dante Gabriel Rossetti (1828-1882) translates the ending:

> Sweet was thy dream; for by that sign, I say,
> Surely the opposite shall come to pass.[58]

---

[57] *Sonnets and Ballate of Guido Cavalcanti*, with translations and an introduction by Ezra Pound (Boston: Small, Maynard & Co., 1912), accessible online: www.sonnets.org/pound.htm/.

[58] *The Collected Works of Dante Gabriel Rossetti* (London: Ellis & Scrutton, 1886), vol. I, 116.

Which still remains obscure. Nevertheless, one can see in Cavalcanti's poem vague outlines of the way Dante's love would progress—the recognition that Beatrice held all value for him and the early intimation that she was mortal and must die. Biographically, Cavalcanti, the older poet, acknowledged the younger and even became Dante's best friend. A. N. Wilson notes that in that day Dante's act of circulating his poem was the equivalent of getting published and receiving reviews.

Just as Aleksandr Pushkin would astonish the poetic elite of St. Petersburg with his teenage opus *Ruslan and Lyudmila* (1817), announcing a genius who would inaugurate a new literature in a new literary language, so more than five centuries earlier Dante accomplished the same feat in Italy. His works led directly to Boccaccio and Italian literature, and in England to Geoffrey Chaucer (c. 1343-1400) and the beginning of English literature. Read *La Fiammetta* by the former and *Troilus and Criysede* by the latter, and you will see the meeting, the glance, the greeting of the *Vita* repeated and developed in realistic and psychological detail.

Given the convention of courtly love, which quickly won literary acceptance, the reader of *La Vita Nuova* might wonder why Dante sought out a screen, a false beloved on whom to turn his attention. Why couldn't he tell Beatrice that he adored her, even though he was betrothed? The answer, only hinted in the text, is that the poet took care to protect the honor of his lady. He could permit no rumor about her among the vulgar, who would not understand the higher form of love. This answer would stand not only for the real situation, which we assume to be Dante Alighieri's love for Beatrice Portinari while he was betrothed, but also for the literary situation, in which both appear to be free. His task was to communicate his devotion to her indirectly, hoping that she would learn of his verse from some other person who read it, at the same time deceiving the screen lady and everyone around him. Needless to say, the ruse was not too gentle to the woman chosen as screen, and, according to his account, it backfired, for Beatrice took it as heartless and denied him her greeting. (Chapters X-XII.)

In addition to protecting her honor, Dante had at least three reasons for keeping his attraction to Beatrice secret. First, Gemma's father, Manetto Donati, might not have been pleased to learn of it; second, Dante's father, Aligiero di Aligiero, might not have been pleased to learn of it; third, Beatrice's father, Folco Portinari, might not have been pleased to learn of it, because he might have already made an arrangement for his offspring as well. Once she was safely married to someone else, it would have been within the bounds of courtly love for Dante to worship her, though still not openly. From his literary account (Chapter XXXIII), it appears that he even hid his love from her brother, who might have served as a go-between. In any case, while he and Gemma were engaged, and Beatrice was not, or even was, any amorous gazes toward her, if noticed by less poetic souls, might have raised eyebrows, wrinkled foreheads and turned down the corners of mouths, after which legal and extremely painful physical repercussions could ensue.

But even this situation was not necessarily exceptional for the time. In an age of clan relationships, arranged marriages and family feuds, when troublemakers were beaten, or tortured, or mutilated, many a young heart must have been broken and trained to sober ways. Dante's father died early in the 1280s, possibly in 1283, the same year in which Dante received Beatrice's greeting. Nevertheless, in 1286, at the age of thirty, as head of the household, duty-bound, Dante married Gemma. The next year, according to Lewis, the first of their three sons, Giovanni, was born. In the same year, 1287, Beatrice married a rich merchant, Simone de' Bardi, and moved away from Dante's neighborhood to the other side of the river Arno. Dante would then have had less chance of seeing her, unless he made a special effort.

However, now that both he and Beatrice were married, any lingering hope that he and she might be together was gone. There was nothing left for him but sublimation. Her greeting would be his bliss. Lewis suggests that the wedding party to which Dante was taken by a friend, described in Chapter XIV, was in fact held in honor of Beatrice.[59] The crushing effect of seeing her in this guise and suffering her laughter at him would be entirely understandable were it so, though it is not obligatory. His sonnet rebuking her for mocking him, followed by two sonnets explaining the power that her appearance had on him, is also consistent with her marriage. Finally, his resolve to write no more about his emotions, but only to sing her praises, and never to speak to her again, makes Lewis' hint a strong supposition. After this point in the narrative, Chapter XVII, there are no more encounters between Dante and Beatrice, and his love for her rises to a "nobler" level.

Again, in the historical world, two years after her marriage, on the last day of 1289, Beatrice's father died. He was a banker, city prior and kindly philanthropist who funded the construction of the Santa Maria Nuova hospital, which still

---

[59] Lewis, *Dante*, 46-48.

stands today on a street named Via Folco Portinari. The grief that his death brought his daughter would have been transmitted to Dante. According to his account, he went and stood outside her house sobbing, but did not see her. Then, only six months later, on 6 June 1290, Beatrice herself died. Now Dante lost even his courtly love and came to a personal crisis.[60]

Wilson mentions, anti-romantically, that during this period Dante did not cease functioning as a healthy married man. Between the years of 1291 and 1296 Gemma gave birth to three children: Pietro, a future lawyer; Iacopo, a future priest; and Antonia, a future nun. In his next work, *The Banquet (Il convivio)*, written between 1304 and 1307, Dante confesses that he was troubled by his attraction to the beautiful lady in the window who took pity on his sobbing for longer than it appears in the *Vita*, and she threatened to take the place of his beloved. It was in the midst of this crisis that he composed his little book, sometime between 1292 and 1295, while children were being born.[61]

For he was a poet, which means someone who knows how to use his emotions and sufferings as literary material. He had kept copies of the poems written about Beatrice and decided to put them together in a new composition. He

---

[60] Lewis 36, 45-46.

[61] A.N.Wilson, chap. XI, loc. 2010-2013 (Kindle edition). Wilson accepts the view of others that the lady in the window could have been Gemma, which strikes me as ridiculous, given that Dante was not just gazing at her without touching, but generating children with her in quick succession. However, Wilson makes a strong case for Dante going back and revising the end of the *Vita* in order to shorten his admitted obsession with the second lady.

would lay them out in sequence and tell the story of how each came to be written, at the same time explaining something about modern poetry in the vernacular and pointing the way to a greater project—the *Commedia*—inspired by the glorious lady. And here is where the exceptional element came in.

In his essays on the art of literature, particularly "On Authorship," Arthur Schopenhauer maintained that the great writer is not the one who finds exotic subjects or impresses readers with arcane research, but the one who takes an everyday theme, the world in front of our eyes, and reveals its meaning. Dante decided, in trying to express his love for Beatrice, to focus on the spark that he felt when he first saw her, the instant of pure love, powerful and inexplicable. This would be the subject of his work. The reader of *La Vita Nuova* may not see it at first, and think the little book to be a quaint love story. But as it goes on, it becomes apparent that something extraordinary is happening, actually something revolutionary. This book is explaining a mystery; it is going to the heart of what we have all felt at the moment of first love, and then, as the case may be, at any such moment thereafter—the incredible, instantaneous spark of love and devotion.

2.

IT IS NOT generally known that the American poet, essayist and transcendental philosopher Ralph Waldo Emerson was an Italianist and afficionado of Dante. From 1839 to 1843 he worked, off and on, on a translation of *La Vita Nuova*; in 1847 he offered his version to a publisher who apparently misplaced it. The manuscript, discovered among Emerson's papers in 1941 and published in the *Harvard Library Bulletin* in 1957, displays a plain and sturdy translation, inherently poetical, that is a delight to read. Had it come out in 1847, Emerson would have had the honor of publishing the first complete translation of the work in the United States. Yet perhaps it is well that it did not, because, being mostly self-taught in the language, he made mistakes, and in addition the original text at his disposal was corrupted. The honor of the first English translation went to Charles Elliot Norton with *The New Life of Dante Alighieri* (Boston, 1867). The famous Dante Gabrieli Rossetti translation came out in 1861.[62]

Among Emerson's enraptured statements about the *Vita*, one jotted down in his journal of 1843 captures the unique quality of the work:

> Dante's *Vita Nuova* reads like the Book of Genesis, as if written before literature, whilst truth yet existed.[63]

Before literature. Before conventions, before interpretation, before we know anything at all. To achieve this effect, Dante strips his account of almost all the particulars in his memory, or, as he calls it, the book of his memory, which means in his day the record of his life that is being kept in heaven. He cuts the dates, the name of the country, the names of the cities, the appearance of the streets and buildings, the family name of his beloved, the color of her

---

[62] J. Chelsey Mathews (ed.), *Dante's VITA NUOVA*, translated by Ralph Waldo Emerson (Chapel Hill: University of North Carolina, 1960), introduction v-xiii.

[63] *Ibid.*, vi.

hair, the color of her eyes, the features of her face, her height, the shape of her body, the shape of her hands, her activities, her relatives (aside from her father and one vaguely defined brother: she had five brothers and five sisters), her social class, her house, her marriage, her husband, any children she may have had, how she spent her time, what she liked to do, how she died; and likewise, as regards himself, his father, his mother, the name of his best friend, the name of his sister (the young woman at his bedside in Chap. XXIII), his education, his occupation, the source of his income, his wife, his children and so on. As regards the unnamed city, Florence, he leaves out the cloth and leather industry, the banking and money-lending, the beatings and killings between families, Corso Donati and his muderous intrigues, the Guelphs and the Ghibellines, the popes and their intrigues. They all become "dogs in the night-time who do not bark," as Wilson puts it.[64] All these particulars he will reserve for scenes in the Inferno, Purgatory and Paradise of the *Commedia*, proof that the attempt to steal back before literature in the *Vita* was a highly conscious design.

Not only the particulars, but also the myriad adjectives and descriptive phrases available to him were cut. To transmit the perfect and unblemished qualities of Beatrice, he resorted again and again to the same words: *gentil, gentilissima, umilia, umile, umilitade,* and so on. These repetitions form a system of classical epithets that simplify the language and point to limits beyond which it cannot go. Once a word for perfection is decided upon, no other word can replace it. Translations may vary these repeated words, but we thought

---

[64] A. N. Wilson, end of chap. 3.

[108]

it best in most instances to stick to the same English equivalents, since Dante had a purpose.

The epithet of Beatrice as *gentile donna* bears within it her tenderness, her untouchableness, her incomparable beauty. Her *umilitade* encompasses her naturalness, her unfeigned kindness, her grace. His reference to her as *gloriosa*, however, always refers to her death—her living in glory. His recollection of perfect love becomes an immaculate walkway of superlative words, iconic images, ritual acts. Were it not for the occasional vivid detail that he inserts into his account it would become sterile, just as a minimalist musical composition can drive one mad until a change of rhythm excites the ear. Such is the precise description of a tremor moving through his body when he sees Beatrice at the wedding party with the fresco running around the walls that he falls back upon. And then wild nightmares and visions, replete with dishevelled women screaming and birds dropping from the sky strike color and terror in the rarefied landscape and reinforce the feeling that we are indeed travelling in a world before historical time.

There is, however, one detail in the account—one missing detail—that strains the border between reality and art. Dante anticipates Beatrice's death by a "false imagining" in Chapter XXIII, so that when death comes in Chapter XXIX it completes a theme and forms a compositional whole. But for the reader caught up in the story, perhaps for every reader, the question of why she died at such an early age forcefully asserts itself. Dante refuses to give an earthly reason, suggesting something miraculous. From his calculations in Chapter XXX it appears that she died when not yet 25. Clearly something went wrong, and Dante remarks it was sudden, yet nearly all his biographers and commentators fail to mention it, or even discuss it, as if dying at age 24 were perfectly normal.

Boccaccio lightly suggests that "a trifle too much cold or heat within us, not to mention countless other accidents and possibilities, easily leads from existence to non-existence." Obviously he overlooked the canzone (second stanza) in Section XXXII of the *Vita* that rules out heat and cold. Lionardo Bruni Aretino (1369-1444) takes issue with Boccaccio on many things, but says nothing about the cause. Lewis says nothing. The commentaries to modern translations say nothing. Wilson suggests complications in childbirth, as good a guess as any.[65]

Despairing of checking every possible book about Dante, Emanuel di Pasquale sent an e-mail request to friends and fellow scholars requesting their knowledge or opinion on the matter. The answers that came back testified perhaps to a number of traditions taught in Italian universities: she died while giving birth to her daughter Francesca, she died from malaria, her husband was a libertine and a debauchee, and so on. All possible, but no one could recall an exact source.

Dante's explains that a report of her death does not fit in with his original design, which he also does not disclose. Yet we can think of a compositional reason why he does not tell us the cause. Having presented Beatrice as the very essence of youthful beauty, grace and love, he could not attribute her death to childbirth without having to reveal that she was a

---

[65] Giovanni Boccaccio, *Vita di Dante*, in Charles Allen Dinsmore, *Aids to the Study of Dante*, 79. Aretino's biography is in the same volume; Wilson, *Dante in Love*, Chapter 10, Kindle location 1928.

married woman, which would at the very least have complicated his design. Likewise, the mention of malaria, if that was the cause, would have weakened the compositional structure, for as it stands the poet damns Morte for taking his lady away, yet allows that God takes her up to heaven, wanting to remove such a gentle soul from such a callous world. He wants, in other words, to curse Death for her cruelty and bless God for his kindness. To reveal the factual cause of Beatrice's death would have shown what God permitted and what Morte did, and thereby introduced material antithetical to the purified scheme of his creation. Especially if there had been suffering, the cause of her death would have sharpened an existing, if only implied, theological discord.

On the other hand, there are a good many critics who hold that the autobiographical element in the *Vita*, in particular Dante's relationship with the historical Beatrice Portinari, is speculative and beside the point; Dante invented the whole thing, whether he referred to a real person or not, and the work should be discussed as his artistic creation independent of biographical material. From this point of view, everything said thus far in this afterword has been absolute hogwash.

It is a fine, formalist view that has its merits, but is unacceptable here, precisely for formalist reasons. The historical traces found in the work form a mosaic, one consistent with the lives of other people as we know them, so it is hard to conceive how the author could have fictionalized the life and character of one historical personage—Beatrice Portinari—whose identity would have been known to others in his time, and not fictionalized the others who are integrated into his work. One character was fictional and the others were real?[66]

One has to consider, for example, that when Dante's daughter Antonia took the veil in 1320 or 1321, the year of his death, she chose the name Sister Beatrice.[67] It is hard to believe that she did so by chance. Did she mean to honor a fictional character or a real woman whom Dante had sainted? Or was "Sister Beatrice, daughter of Dante Alighieri," as a document of 1371 names her, someone other than Antonia? The view here is that it requires more invention to discount the historical Beatrice than to accept her as the prototype for Dante's immortal beloved. With her, as with the other biographical and historical facts, such as those concerning her father, the pieces fall into place.

In his famous essay on Dante, T. S. Eliot considers the problem and concludes that neither side—pure fiction vs. pure autobiography—can be definitely proven. In Eliot's admittedly unprovable view, Dante had an experience that he considered significant, not just for himself, but for others. And so he wrote it up in allegorical form, in accordance with the mentality of his time. It is an *allegory*, says Eliot, and therefore cannot be classified as either truth or fiction.[68]

In a similar vein, Charles Singleton writes most compellingly that the reason Dante wrote the prose commentary to his poems about Beatrice was to prove that she was a

---

[66] See Wilson, *Dante in Love*, Chapter XV, Kindle location 3431; and Barbara Reynolds, "Introduction" to her translation *Dante, Vita Nuova (Poems of Youth)* (New York: Penguin Books, 1969), 11-25.

[67] Lewis, *Dante: A Life*, 165.

[68] T. S. Eliot, "Dante" (1929), *Selected Essays* (NY: Harcourt, Brace Jovanovich, 1960), 199-237.

miracle—not a poetic trope, but an actual miracle. Hence the numerological calculations to show that she was always accompanied by the number nine, and the outright statement in Chapter XXX that she was in fact identical to number nine—an incarnation of the holy trinity. Hence the poems portraying her miraculous effects on others and, of course, the purifying effect of her greeting. Hence the reason she died—God and all the saints in heaven wanted her. The point here is not that we should believe these things, though Singleton does, but that Singleton puts his finger on Dante's design: Dante believed these things.[69]

Some critics would have it that autobiography in itself is fiction, but this is surely not so, no more than biography or history are fiction. The author of each genre must make countless choices when deciding what to include in his account. He may strive to be absolutely honest or to slant his view the way he thinks best; in either event, he will betray a bias, unintentional in the first case and intentional in the second. The reality is that no one can possess all the facts of his own life, the life of another or the life of a people, and there is always more than one way of handling the available facts. Only in the mind of God can there be omniscience and perfect truth, and yet even a poet who believed in the mind of God could exclude almost all the details from his autobiographical account in his desire to reveal the pure truth.

A feminist and not only a feminist might say that Dante drained Beatrice of blood and put her on a pedestal. He never saw her, or at least never described her, as a real, live,

---

[69] Charles Southward Singleton, *An Essay on the Vita Nuova* (1949), (Harvard University Press, 1958, reprinted by John Hopkins University Press, 1977), chapter one: "The Death of Beatrice."

flesh-and-blood woman. Which is true. But such was not his intention, and such a view, though valid from one perspective, would miss another. For example, the tragic portrait of Francesca and Paolo, the young lovers whom the literary persona of Dante sees trapped forever in Hell. It is not just an isolated story, but an allegory linked to the *Vita*.

In Canto V of the *Inferno*, Francesca tells the character Dante what happened, how she could not resist the urging of her *cor gentil*; how she fell in love with Paolo, the brother of her husband Giovanni, and while reading a romance together with him allowed him to kiss her. Giovanni rushed in and stabbed them both to death. Upon hearing the story, Dante the character faints dead away. Commentators on the *Commedia* note that Francesca da Rimini (1255-1285) was a real-life contemporary of Dante, and her fate presented him with a moral of the wrong direction his relationship with Beatrice might have taken. The point is emphasized when the figure of Beatrice appears at the end of his fictional journey through Hell and chastises him for pursuing false pleasures after her death, then leads him up to Paradise.[70]

As Eliot points out, it takes an effort to see Dante in his own time. We are inclined to see the story of his love for Beatrice through the filter of the literature that has come after him, and after Emerson as well. We have either read it or imbibed it with our mother's milk, or with our super-

---

[70] See, for example, the commentary of Lewis, 106-109, 156-159. Francesca da Rimini has been the inspiration for numerous musical compositions, notably by Tchaikovsky, Rachmaninoff and Arthur Foote; and works of art, notably by Ingres, Doré and Joseph Noel Paton, whose painting of Dante dreaming of Francesca and Paolo graces the cover of this book.

market baby formula. Mention Copericus, Newton, Rousseau, Darwin and Freud, and you transform the very grounds for thinking about human beings, love and sex.

To read Dante is to go back before an infinite, impersonal, self-regulating universe, biological instincts and psychological motivations. Dante cannot think that he is programmed by his DNA, driven by his hormones, conditioned by his social conventions. He must refer to medieval conceptions of the body, numerological calculations of predetermined meetings, theological definitions of the holy trinity, prophetic dreams, visions. He feels love with an impact not mediated by scientific knowledge, laboratory experiments and a mass-media entertainment complex bombarding the population with digitalized white flashes transmitted by orbiting satellites 24/7. In his time the mechanical clock had just been invented. A little flash, a glint, pierces him, and he has all the information he needs.

He spells out his interpretation of love in *The Banquet*, a flawed and incomplete work, in which he attempts to explain everything he knows and everything he aims to do by means of Aristotelian logic. Here, for those who like to see the clockwork behind the poetic face, is a typical passage about the divine spark:

> ... Each form in some way has the essence of the Divine Nature in itself; not that the Divine Nature can be divided and communicated to these, but participated in by these, almost in the same way that the other stars participate in the nature of the Sun. And the nobler the form, the more does it retain of that Divine Nature.

[115]

Wherefore the human Soul, which is the noblest form of all those which are generated under Heaven, receives more from the Divine Nature than any other. [...] And since its existence depends upon God, and is preserved by him, it naturally desires and longs to be united to God, and so add strength to its own being. And since, in the goodness of Human Nature, Reason gives us proof of the Divine, it follows that, naturally, the Human Soul is united therewith by the path of the spirit so much the sooner, and so much the more firmly, in proportion as those good qualities appear more perfect; which appearance of perfection is achieved according as the power of the Soul to produce a good impression is strong and clear, or is trammelled and obscure. And this union is that which we call Love, whereby it is possible to know that which is within the Soul, by looking at those whom it loves in the world without. This Love, which is the union of my Soul with that gentle Lady in whom so much of the Divine Light was revealed to me, is that speaker of whom I speak; since from him continuous thoughts were born, whilst gazing at and considering the wondrous power of this Lady who was spiritually made one with my Soul.[71]

---

[71] Dante Alighieri, *The Banquet (Il Convito)*, translated by Elizabeth Price Sayer (1887), Public Domain Books (2006), The Third Treatise, Chapter Two, Kindle edition, location 1059-1071. It is not entirely clear in this passage whether Dante is speaking of his first love (Beatrice) or second (the Lady in the Window), but the principle is the same.

These concepts, or at least their formulations, are all pretty much outlived. Today we are inclined to turn to psychology to understand the Beatrice experience. Freud's dissident colleague, Carl Gustav Jung (1875-1961), wrote of woman as seer and guide for man in the process of his self-discovery and self-realization—a process Jung termed individuation. He described the impact of what he called the feminine archetype—the Anima—hidden in the psyche of the unsuspecting male and awakened by the glint of an eye seen for an instant. The road ahead may be rough, and even lead to obsession and psychopathology, but Jung sketched out four stages a man might follow in a successful venture: Eve, the instinctual and biological woman; Faust's Helen, the romantic and esthetic woman; the Virgin Mary, who raises love to a purely spiritual plane; and Sapientia or Lady Philosophy, who awakens wisdom. These stages were meant to be suggestive and not to apply to every case or even to a single case, yet they indicated the endurance of a spiritual and even mystical element in the scientific age. The final stage of individuation for Jung is a rapprochement with reality, a cessation of self-induced obsession and suffering, and a new state of self-sufficiency in which the opposite sex is seen as human—both good and bad, but still potentially lovable.[72]

Dante's course is to trace the spark of love to its source, which in his view, as we have seen, must be the highest and therefore divine. Beatrice in her essence must be divine, the

---

[72] A colorful account is given in C. G. Jung, Marie-Louise von Franz et al, *Man and His Symbols* (New York: Doubleday, 1964), 177-188 ("The Anima: The Woman Within") & 189-195 ("The Animus: The Man Within").

very word we use for beauty whether or not we attach it to a religious belief. Every little girl can catch us off guard and make us think she is divine; every beautiful woman too; and in fact every woman when she is beautiful. Dante, by taking us back before literature, permits us to feel the truth of that moment, which is both rapturous and profoundly disturbing, because in every instance the divine one is mortal. His purpose in retaining that moment is to make it instructive and to bring us to God. Those of us who won't be brought to an invisible, mute and motionless God must endure love and mortality with a sense of universal injustice.

3.

DANTE IS classical, medieval and renaissance at the same time. Classical in his esteem for Homer, Aristotle and Virgil; medieval in his convoluted meditations on the power of numbers (numerology), the stars (astrology) and heaven (Catholicism). He is renaissance in his decision to look deeply into an emotion, to develop its expression in the "vulgar language" and to submit his work to others for examination. He is romantic, of course, in his prolonged description of his love, his melancholy, his grief. He is realist in his admission that his attraction to the woman in the window was becoming sexual and threatening to supplant his love for his deceased beloved. He is idealist in forcing himself to reject this attraction and hold forever to the one ideal woman, whose goodness will improve the universe. He is modern in creating this autobiographical work by excluding details from his life that would detract from the effect that he wants, as he reveals in the *Convivio*. He is universal in constructing years later an epic, a poetic monument—*La*

Commedia, which later generations called *La Divina Commedia*—that will color the conception of Christianity and influence mankind with a mythic quest for knowledge and redemption, taking an ancient pagan (Virgil) as guide through the underworld and the divine feminine (Beatrice) as Christian guide into paradise. All this is adumbrated in this *libello*, this simple little book drawn from some poems and selective memory called *La Vita Nuova*.

The original intention of the present translation was to make it modern, colloquial and easy to read. This intention could not be realized, however, without fundamentally altering the work. A colloquial paraphrase could do it, but a faithful rendition—never. From the very first words, referring to the rotation of the sun around the earth and the author's obsession with the number nine, it was clear that the medieval element had to be retained and at least briefly explained. A paraphrase or popularization would result in a comic-book version.

Likewise the sentence structure. You just can't smooth it out. In a preface to his translation, Mark Musa writes amusingly of Dante's prose: "The reader always seems to be in the midst of a dependent clause, or to have just escaped from one, or to be about to enter into another." And yet Musa decides: "it would be a sacrilege to reduce Dante's elaborate prose periods to simpler predications."[73] Indeed, it can't be otherwise, because once you start to fool with Dante's sentences, which are tightly wrought, you begin to dismantle the work. For better or for worse, we had to be faithful to the text, which means stick to a fairly literal translation,

---

[73] Dante Alighieri, *Vita Nuova*, translated by Mark Musa (New York: Oxford University Press, 1991, 1999), "Note on the Translation," xxii.

[119]

retaining its mixed ancient, medieval and modern elements, trying always to keep it as light and accessible as possible by choosing English words and idioms not too modern and not too remote.

The *Vita* has been translated many times before, each time in a different way, as each new translator solves the problems of its prose and its poetry, and tries to bring it more freshly and directly to the reader of the day. As with every classic, each translator checks the work of his or her predecessors, though usually without mentioning it, as can be seen from a careful comparison of the various texts. When one translation influences another, it is not a matter of cribbing or stealing, but of recognizing a solution that is correct and cannot be improved upon. Most often the influence is the reverse: the predecessor seems wrong or inadequate, and the newcomer strives to better him. And as with every classic, and also religious texts, there are passages that have not been decisively solved by anyone and remain moot. Consequently, every translation makes different interpretations, emphases and choices.

The present translation offers a few novelties. First, the epithets attached to Beatrice, and sometimes to other ladies, are translated the same way almost every time. If Dante says *la gentilissima donna,* and we translate the phrase "the most gracious lady," we will do so almost every time he uses that phrase, not seeking to add variety to the narrative with an alternate translation. Only on occasion, when the text suggested a different coloration, such as *fair lady,* was a change allowed. The words *umile* ("meek, humble") and *umilitade* ("humility") are used expansively by Dante, indicating that they had much broader meanings in his day than in ours, so the translations of them had to be varied. But as a rule, the epithets are set.

Second, the personifications of Love and Death are emphasized by retaining the original Italian names capitalized by Dante. It is easier, we feel, for an English reader to imagine someone named "Amore" to be dressed as a wayfarer walking along the road than someone named "Love." The same applies to "Morte"—"Death." Of course, everyone knows who they are.

Third, we tried a new way of rendering the verse, which requires a brief explanation. The meters and rhyme schemes of Dante's *sonnets, canzoni* and *ballad* are quite involved, as indicated in the note on the translation at the beginning of this volume. Those translations that attempt to retain both the meter and rhyme, such as by Norton and Rossetti, are forced to paraphrase in order to find English rhymes appropriate to the sense, and then to rearrange words and sometimes whole lines in order to put the rhyming words in the right place. The result may be flowing and even pleasurable, but the degree of divergence from the original text is extreme.

Blank-verse translations—iambic pentameter without rhyme—fare better than rhyming versions in retaining the meaning, but even they are forced to add words in order to produce eleven syllables, so that all sorts of padding may occur, especially when the Italian words in a given instance have more syllables than their English equivalents. Thus we get lots of little inserted words that Dante did not write—*such, so, now, and, my, yet, only, still, dear, sweet*—and often two or three English words for one Italian word, and once again paraphrases.

[121]

Our option was to adopt blank verse—no rhyme—without insisting on five beats per line. If five beats come naturally—good. If rhymes come naturally—good. If only four beats, or even three—good enough. Generally, however, we wanted at least four. Even in this lenient scheme, distortions can occur. In order to produce a steady stream of unstressed and stressed syllables, ta-TA, ta-TA, ta-TA, choices of words must be made on the basis of their stress: *in/within, on/upon, get/obtain, say/declare, weep/lament,* and so on. However, these same choices are made in iambic pentameter blank verse. Our version, not insisting on pentameter, is essentially blank verse without padding and paraphrase; it loses the symmetry of a guaranteed five beats per line, but retains the rhythm and the sense.

La Vita Nuova is very much a period piece, like a harpsichord partita by Bach that is played again and again by different performers who more or less hit the same keys, yet bring each audience a new experience. We hope that we have brought the work to a new audience without hitting too many clinkers. As for me, a new Dante enthusiast, I hope that my afterword has answered a few questions, provoked many more and encouraged the reader to seek out the profound studies of the true Dante scholars, several of whom are listed below.

Selected titles for further reading:

Benedetto Croce, *The Poetry of Dante,* translated by Douglas Ainslie (New York: Paul P. Appel, 1971).

T. S. Eliot, "Dante" (1929), *Selected Essays* (NY: Harcourt, Brace Jovanovich, 1960), 199-237.

W. B. Lewis, *Dante: A Life* (New York: Penguin, 2009).

Barbara Reynolds, *Dante: The Poet, The Political Thinker, The Man* (London: I. B. Tauris, 2006). *

Charles Southward Singleton, *An Essay on the Vita Nuova* (1949), (Harvard University Press, 1958, reprinted by John Hopkins University Press, 1977).

Charles Williams, *The Figure of Beatrice: A Study in Dante* (New York, Noonday Press, 1961; reprinted by Acrophile Press, 2005).

A. N. Wilson, *Dante in Love* (New York: Farrar, Straus & Giroux, 2011).

For a fascinating and sometimes amusing look at how others read *La Vita Nuova*, go the website called "Good Reads." The address:

http://www.goodreads.com/book/show/540422.Vita_Nuova/.

EMANUEL DI PASQUALE was born in Ragusa, Sicily, and emigrated to America in 1957. His translations from Italian include *The Journey Ends Here* by Carlo della Corte (Gradiva, 2000), *Sharing a Trip* by Silvio Ramat (Bordighera Press, 2001), which won a Raiziss/dePalchi Fellowship from the Academy of American Poets, and *Between the Blast Furnaces and the Dizziness* by Milo De Angelis (Chelsea Editions, 2003). He has published sixteen books of his own poetry, the first being *Genesis* (Boa Editions,1989); and the last two being *Siciliana* (2009) and *Harvest* (2011), both from Bordighera Press. He has also written a book for children, *Cartwheel to the Moon* (Cricket Books, 2003). He lives by the ocean in Long Branch, New Jersey.

BRUNO ALEMANNI was born in Washington DC and pursued Cold War studies in several countries before turning to other languages and alternative philosophies. Long employed in anonymous bibliographical and archival work, he wrote reports for a limited number of specialists and methodologists before beginning his study of Dante. The Afterword is the first work published in his own name—the work, he says, of "an enthusiast." He is retired and lives in a remote and virtually uninhabited area of the Chihuahua Desert.